GENERATI♻N
GREEN

Other Simon Pulse nonfiction titles you might enjoy

In Their Shoes: Extraordinary Women
Describe Their Amazing Careers
Deborah Reber

The Social Climber's Guide to High School
Robyn Schneider

Click! The Girl's Guide to Knowing What
You Want and Making It Happen
Annabel Monaghan and Elisabeth Wolfe

Chill: Stress-Reducing Techniques for a More
Balanced, Peaceful You
Deborah Reber

GENERATI♻N
GREEN

The Ultimate Teen Guide
to Living an Eco-Friendly Life

WRITTEN BY LINDA SIVERTSEN AND TOSH SIVERTSEN

SIMON PULSE
New York   London   Toronto   Sydney

SIMON PULSE

An imprint of Simon & Schuster Children's Publishing Division

1230 Avenue of the Americas, New York, NY 10020

Copyright © 2008 by Linda Sivertsen and Tosh Sivertsen

Excerpt from *Straight from the Horse's Mouth* by Amelia Kinkade.

Copyright © 2001 by Amelia Kinkade. Published by New World
Library, Novato, CA, and used by permission.

SIMON PULSE and colophon are registered trademarks of
Simon & Schuster, Inc.

Designed by Jane Archer

The text of this book was set in Gotham

Manufactured in the United States of America

First Simon Pulse edition August 2008

10 9 8 7 6 5 4

Library of Congress Control Number 2008922275

ISBN-13: 978-1-4169-6122-2

ISBN-10: 1-4169-6122-4

*In loving memory of Al and Joanne Tisch—
Dad and Mom, Grandpa and Grandma.
It's because of you that we know what we know,
care like we do, and even attempt to
make a difference. May we do you proud.*

C♺NTENTS

you are generation **green**!

hen I was a kid, I didn't know that we were more environmentally conscious—greener— than my friends' families. I just thought everybody lived like we did, and there weren't a whole lot of other people around to tell me otherwise. From age four until I was nine my parents raised me in the woods in northern New Mexico, where we lived on hundreds of acres of raw land. My folks built our house themselves, which was 100 percent solar-powered. (Mom even juiced her laptop from the sun.) We lived "off the grid," meaning we weren't connected to the electrical system or public utilities. We didn't need an alarm clock; we just went to sleep after it got dark and woke up with the sun. It was so far away from everything that friends always got lost trying to find us down the maze of dirt roads. I loved it, even though we had so few of the things most kids take for granted—working toilets, indoor heating, phones, trash pickup, a dishwasher. If we wanted water, we couldn't just turn on a faucet; we had to catch it from the roof—did you know you can save hundreds of gallons from a single summer afternoon's storm?—or lug it in five-gallon jugs from a well a quarter of a mile away. Water was so precious we'd even catch the morning dew in our tank.

As a five-year-old I used to help my folks chop up dead wood for heat with a small ax. That was a blast, and I never even got a nick. When my friends visited, Mom would take us on treasure hunts, looking for deer and moose tracks, and arrowheads. That was all great, but I had to use an outhouse for *forever*, which was a total drag. We had empty jars stored under the kitchen sink that we used for those "late night" emergencies when I didn't want to go outside in the pitch-dark and walk the thirty feet in the freezing cold to use the outhouse. And without a heater (can you say 22 degrees in the living room at three a.m.?) if I used one of those jars in the middle of the night in the wintertime, by morning the contents were often frozen. Okay, pretty gross, I know. T.M.I.

Living in a forest and being so close to nature changes you. I used to run for hours in the woods with my siblings—ha, really my pack of dogs—so townspeople called me Mowgli the Jungle Boy. Sometimes I'd put newborn puppies into my pockets to keep them warm while I went out walking in the snow. Life in New Mexico taught me so many things. Like how precious our natural resources are. You become a homegrown expert in low-impact living because being even a little wasteful in that environment feels all wrong—like wearing a tuxedo to a hip-hop concert. Some things just don't go together.

We bought our land from a Native-American medicine man who lived in a small makeshift cabin nearby. We lived next to his tepee and his *inepi*—an igloo-shaped contraption where he did these amazing sweat lodge ceremonies. The medicine man taught us to "walk lightly" on Mother Earth and ponder the thoughts of plants and rocks, "who had seen so much." He taught us to think about how everything we do affects future generations— perhaps the most important lesson passed down to him from his elders. It's easier to learn that lesson when you're surrounded by grass and brown earth and can literally see your own footprints.

We saw so many different approaches to caring for the earth in rural New Mexico—but also so many contradictions. The medicine man said that he wanted nothing but a can of beans every day and a tepee to live in, and that he dreamed of going totally back to nature— but when he got a gas generator, he always had his TV blaring the news. The *consique* (tribal spiritual leader) of the Taos Pueblo, "Grampa" Pete Concha, told us he feared for our safety every time we went to "the outworld"—Los Angeles, where Mom and Dad had to go for work (Mom's a writer and Dad's an actor). But wasn't our favorite city also sacred by just being part of the earth? I was confused. When we first moved to New Mexico, the locals didn't immediately trust our good intentions, calling us "Hollywood" and "Easy Money" and "Indian Wannabes." We had to work hard to fit in and convince them that we cared about the land and their ways as much as they did. Sometimes it felt like we were living in two worlds.

When I was in fourth grade, we moved back to a suburb of Los Angeles so my dad could be closer to his acting auditions and Mom could do press for her first book. Then I really *did* have to figure out how to live in two worlds! I remember being psyched about the running water—turning the faucet in the bathroom on and off . . . how totally easy! It was around that time I quickly figured out that, unlike my dad, I was a city dude and loved living a more comfortable lifestyle. Flush toilets are the shizz! Mom and I are more alike in that way, but we're so grateful for our years living in the forest, for the seasons we spent living simply in the middle of so much natural beauty. It's too remote for more than brief visits right now, but that experience stays with you no matter where you go, kind of the way I imagine taking a long safari in Africa would. Or going to the moon.

Each day I find myself playing a balancing act in both of my lives. I love the best of what our modern world provides (like indoor toilets and heaters), but I don't want to stress out the planet to live my life.

I'm guessing you're doing that same balancing act. You're worried about pollution and global warming and running out of resources, but you also love your five pairs of designer jeans and daily custom-built Frappuccinos. I feel ya. And maybe it seems like global warming and other world problems are so big and "out there" that they barely touch you—and it's not like you'll ever live on a melting glacier. But really, those problems and their ripple effects are closer than you think.

For instance, do you love going to the beach? If so, have you noticed the litter? Here on the West Coast they're always closing the beaches because bacteria-laden raw sewage keeps showing up in the water. Ugh, is anything more disgusting? According to the Natural Resources Defense Council, sewage spills and overflows caused 1,301 national beach closing and advisory days in 2006. Another fourteen thousand closing and advisory days were due to unknown sources of pollution. Ugh. On a good day you're cruising along the shore looking for seashells and you find a ton of plastic bottles instead. It's not only gross, but it's bad news, because those plastics don't biodegrade. They just break down into tinier and tinier pieces until they turn into a kind of toxic dust that the fish eat—and then we eat the fish! Some scientists think there are six times as many of these microplastics in the oceans as plankton, which is one of the most important food supplies to aquatic life.

If you're not into the beach, maybe you love skiing or snowboarding. You can see signs of the ripple effects there, too. Thanks to rising global temperatures and record droughts, the snowpacks are often weak and unpredictable, and the ski season can end before it even seems to get rolling. Perhaps you have asthma, and pollution is making you wheeze? Or you're sick of all the rain. Or you aren't getting enough rain. Or you just want to go play sports without sucking down thick brown air. Maybe you live on the coast and everyone around you is nervous. It makes you wonder if the house you grew up in will be on dry land by the time you have your own kids.

So maybe it's starting to hit home that all this environmental stuff isn't really "out there." It's right in our own backyards, all around us. It's hard to believe, but while we were working on this very book, Mom and I had to pack up two cars' worth of our belongings and our dogs and cat in an hour and flee a raging wildfire at the top of our hill. And then, as we were finishing up the last chapters, Mom got stuck in the middle of a storm with eighty-five-mile-an-hour hurricane winds! It's as though Mother Nature's trying to make a statement here—as if to warn us that she needs our cooperation! I've been reading about how fires and hurricanes and other extreme weather events are indications that the environment is stressed out, out of balance. Sure seems so. It's really gotten me thinking even more about what my friends and I can do to lighten our impact.

A lot of people think that teens are too self-involved to care about global issues. Sure, if your dad and mom are fighting or your ex–best friend is going out with your ex or your family cat just had to be put to sleep or you flunked your last math test, okay, you're going to worry more about that stuff than about a melting glacier thousands of miles away. At least for that day or week or month.

But that doesn't mean we don't care. I'm convinced we do. We're just not sure what to do next. My mom and I have a theory. We think both teens *and* adults are waiting to be asked to do more. We're expecting someone in power to ask us to step up, to sacrifice for the greater good. Like the Greatest Generation did during WWII when people rationed everything they used. Back in the 1940s people really appreciated the smallest things and found uses for everything. (My grandma took the burlap from flour sacks and made them into dish towels—can you imagine?) I think teens today are just as willing to do our part; maybe we simply need a little more information and a little more motivation.

So that's why Mom and I are doing this book; it's our way of inviting everyone to step up and become our own Greatest Generation: *Generation Green*. We may not have gotten ourselves into this mess, but let's face it, our elders are hoping we find the solutions. So let's do it. Let's surprise everyone. Do you have anything better to do? Okay, don't answer that. Video games and texting BFFs don't count!

This book can help you get started. You'll be reading about a lot of different ideas here that you may not have heard before. We're not scientists, but we're passionate and a bit wacky, and we love to research and write about all the options. We'll introduce you to teens and several celebrity friends who are doing some really great things for the environment, as well as people we just find very inspiring. We'll share our favorite tips for greener living, ideas that can help you change your family, your town, or even a law or two. Whether you want to lead your family in green style, or organize group events at your school (hey, not bad on the college applications), or just do a little more to do your part, you'll find it here. It's a big world, and there's a lot to cover!

As you read on, maybe think about the person you might want to become for the rest of your rockin' and hopefully *very* long life! Think about what kind of contributions you could make, both large and small—at home and in the world. There are so many tiny, creative steps you can take every day to lessen your impact on the earth. Like wrapping a friend's present in newspaper comics instead of buying expensive gift wrap that gobbles up resources and energy in order to make it. Or like taking your lunch to school in a cool vintage lunch box you scored on eBay instead of tossing out another paper or plastic baggie. Or holding on to your cell phone a little longer instead of automatically upgrading to the hippest model and relegating your old one to a landfill somewhere (even though we know you'd recycle yours!).

Ask yourself what kind of career could you go into that would fill a valuable need (maybe even make you a hero) and set you up for a great life? If you have no idea, keep reading, because as temperatures skyrocket, water tables drop, sea levels rise, populations expand, and pollution worsens, ingenuity, technologies, and a gazillion job opportunities will emerge that you'd never have thought up in your craziest, most whacked-out imaginative moments. Or maybe you *will* think of them. . . .

There'll be some big bumps in the road, no doubt. But the possibilities, too, are endless. Although it can be tempting, I don't want to go into denial and hide in my room playing Final Fantasy with the best of them. No, I don't intend to go down so easily. Because I've seen with my own eyes how little changes add up to big changes.

Guess I've got Mom to thank for that. She's kind of a maniac about all this stuff; she's definitely the only mom I know who takes the green water out of the salad spinner every night—from lettuce she grows in our backyard—and waters the houseplants with it. Her mother, my Grams, used to water their yard with recycled laundry water. When it rained, their front lawn would be covered in suds. How embarrassing is that? Sometimes I just have to shake my head. I've never seen anyone else in the whole world air-dry old recycled paper towels and use them to pick up dog poop on a walk. I'm not as gung ho as she is, but I've adopted some of her cooler habits. I'm working hard on myself to live a greener life, and hopefully I can influence others by my example. If you do that too, how tight would that be? We'll all watch this thing turn around together.

The important thing is, we've got to be patient with ourselves. Don't pressure yourself. You've already got enough stress up in your grill—no doubt. Here's the thing: You're used to school, where there aren't a lot of do-overs unless your parents write you a major note. You blow a test or bomb a paper, and you don't always get a second chance. Same with striking out in the big game. But this isn't the SATs or the baseball championships—no one's keeping score. In the real world, there are a lot of second chances. And here's the thing about being green: It's *never* all or nothing. Every day you can start again, make other choices—better ones. If you have to buy a bottle of water because you forgot your "eco" version from home, just reuse the plastic bottle a few times and recycle it when you're done. Every little thing you do matters. Your goal is to make small changes you can stick with, not to go bat-guano crazy trying to do everything green and then burn out in a week.

I think that's why Mom doesn't get mad when I space out and forget to unplug my cell phone charger, or drive a mile somewhere instead of taking my bike, or toss clean clothes into the hamper because I didn't feel like hanging them up and they got dirty on the floor. She gets that sometimes it takes a while for a new green habit to sink in, and that we just need to keep trying and we'll get there.

And she's taught me not to be a "green bore" either—lecturing my friends about how they shouldn't do something. I did that once with my buds when they littered out the car window one day and I was so mad we nearly got into a fistfight! It took us two very tense days to get over it. Just walk your talk. Your buddies will come around. Mine have.

One day at a time. Just do what you can, and that's cool. It gets easier as you go. If we're all doing little things, day in and day out it will really add up, even if we're not perfect. It's all good.

Mom and I hope this book will inspire you to do what we're doing: to try our best to see the world with new eyes. Green eyes. So, take the stories, tips, suggestions, facts, and ideas laid out here and let them sink in and reframe your vision, like colored contact lenses. And visit our website, www.generationgreenthebook.com, often for new, updated, fun information on what teens like you are doing to green up their lives. And write to us and let us know how it's going—what cool ideas you come up with. Maybe we'll profile you on our site, or include a story about you in our next book!

Green out!

TOSH SIVERTSEN
Los Angeles, California
18 years old

CHAPTER ONE

GREEN MACHINE

et's face it, when we turn on the tap, we want to get clean water every time, not something that looks like a cross between green tea yogurt and coffee sludge. When we flick the switch, we want power for our lights, video games, and TVs. When we turn the key in the ignition, we expect the car to roar to life. We're locked into so many systems to live our busy lives. It's like we live in a big machine made up of a zillion parts, and they all have to work together or the machine will break down or, worse yet, grind to a complete halt. We depend on our green machine, the environment, for so much more than the conveniences we take for granted; we don't seem to truly appreciate that our earth's health and our own health are completely connected. When the earth gets sick, we get sick too.

Unfortunately, there's a lot of evidence that our green machine is breaking down and that the earth is getting sicker. Each year seems to bring on more dramatic natural events—surpassing all previous records. A heat wave in Europe in the summer of 2003 killed thirty-five thousand people. The December 26, 2004, tsunami in the Indian Ocean killed more than three hundred thousand people. Hurricane Katrina was seven times more destructive than any other natural storm in our history, and killed more than eighteen hundred people. The Southern California wildfires of October 2007 forced hundreds of thousands of people to flee their homes—making it the largest evacuation in California history.

The planet seems to be running a fever, too. The year 2005 was the warmest year in recorded history—until 2006, which became the warmest year on record—until 2007, which quickly surpassed 2006 as of April, and then continued throughout December as the warmest year on record.

Maybe you're thinking, *Hey, that's okay. I like warm weather, so what's the problem?* Those higher temperatures are causing animal and plant extinctions; failed crops; lower water tables; drying wells, creeks, and rivers; disappearing lakes; a decrease in snowpack and glaciers worldwide; and longer, scarier fire seasons.

It's a big world, but we're using it up. Georgia had such a severe water shortage in the fall of 2007 that the governor led a prayer vigil for rain. (Our Native-American friends weren't at all surprised when the state got rain the next day.) In fact, water shortages are an international crisis. We're destroying our rain forests so quickly that if we don't do something fast, by 2030 there will be only 10 percent of them left. Even the skies over our heads are disappearing with the depletion of the ozone layer. What's the deal here?

With all the evidence that our green machine is breaking down, is it too late to fix it? It's easy to think that all our global problems are so big that there's no solution, so why even bother to do anything? We'll tell you why: because people *are* identifying what's causing the problems, they *are* finding solutions, the solutions *are* working, and individuals like you *do* make a difference.

The key here is that we all need to think big—be part of a large national or international effort—*and* think small— act more thoughtfully and locally as individual teens. One person can and does make a difference—but think of how much more powerful and effective we'll be when we pull together! It all starts with understanding how, why, and where the green machine is breaking down.

This chapter will give you the basic lowdown on some of the most important issues affecting our planet, followed by a sampling of the kinds of innovative solutions people are employing to fix these problems. We think that if you have the inside scoop on what's going wrong and what it'll take to turn it around, you'll be more pumped about trying some of the suggestions to come. If you want to delve even deeper into any of these topics, we've listed some of our favorite books in the Resources section at the back of this book.

climate change

The biggest evidence that our green machine is breaking down is the dramatic way our climate has changed over the last few decades. The most ominous change, of course, is global warming, which has contributed to every one of the catastrophic problems we've already mentioned. In fact, some scientists think the term "global warming" sounds too pleasant and recommend we use a new term, "climate disruption," so people really understand how chaotic the problem is. Laurie David, who produced Al Gore's groundbreaking Oscar-winning documentary, *An Inconvenient Truth,* calls global warming "the mother of all issues," and that makes sense because if Mama Earth ain't happy, no one's happy. Since this is the big fajita, we're going to spend more of our time on this one.

Global warming refers to the fact that worldwide temperatures are rising, both on land and sea, and are expected to continue to go up over time—even if we completely stop contributing to the problem this very minute.

Why is this happening? Because a normal process has gone out of whack. Normal heating of the earth results when the sun's rays hit our planet, warming the land, vegetation, and oceans. The heat then radiates back toward outer space. So-called greenhouse gases (made up largely of carbon dioxide and methane) in our atmosphere act like a blanket to trap the warm air from escaping into the great beyond. This blanket is what makes our planet so special. Ahhhh. Like flowers in a greenhouse, we're protected and live a mostly cozy existence. Without this protective layer, we'd freeze.

This atmosphere of ours allows our global temperatures to remain "just right"—what scientists call the Goldilocks Principle—unlike any other place we know of in the universe. Venus has a massive blanket trapping its heat, contributing to its hellishly hot 900 degree temperature. Mars, at the other end of the spectrum, has a very thin blanket, making it an unbearably cold -220 degrees. Earth is the only planet so far in all of the known universes with this fragile range of temperatures that fosters life for many millions of species. Our perfect blanket is all we've got between the harsh reality of space and us.

Most scientists believe that we're accelerating the process of global warming because, for example, we're burning more and more fossil fuels (oil, gas, and coal) and wood, producing more greenhouse gases such as carbon dioxide, and therefore trapping more and more heat in our atmosphere. Increased global warming means that our protective blanket is becoming stifling, and if the process continues, the situation will be a nightmare. Living on Earth will feel like being forced to stay under the heaviest down comforter while wearing flannel pajamas and wool socks on the hottest summer night.

All that extra heat is melting the glaciers and ice caps, which hold the majority of frozen freshwater on the planet. Scientists conservatively estimate that because of global warming the sea level could rise anywhere from eight to thirty-eight inches by the next century. While that may not sound like a huge difference, in fact, more than one hundred million people live within a yard or so of sea level, which means that all those people could lose their homes.

Imagine all the homes and businesses located along the twelve thousand miles of coastline in America—flooded!

Ten percent of all the world's land is covered with glacial ice. According to the National Snow and Ice Data Center (NSIDC), if every glacier in the world melted today (which some say could also happen within this century, depending on what we do or don't do), the oceans would rise about two hundred thirty feet!

Global warming affects another protective element over our heads: the ozone layer. This very thin layer, located primarily in the earth's stratosphere, absorbs almost all the harmful ultraviolet rays from the sun. The greater the global warming, the cooler the stratosphere becomes, which may be related to even greater destruction of the ozone layer. Wait. How can global warming *cool* the stratosphere? Because greenhouse gases trap heat from the planet that would naturally rise, warming the troposphere and cooling the stratosphere, according to climatologist Ben Santer of Lawrence Livermore National Laboratory, part of the U.S. Department of Energy. Scientists know that the destruction was accelerated by the release of certain man-made substances such as chlorofluorocarbons (CFCs), found in some aerosols, industrial cleaners, and the Freon used in refrigeration, which we'll discuss below. The depletion of the ozone formed holes around the north and south poles. The result? More ultraviolet rays reach the earth, which means more humans suffer from sunburn and skin cancer—further proof of the connection between our health and the earth's.

Global warming doesn't affect only the temperature of our planet; it affects the storms all around the world, turning them more violent. Globally the number of hurricanes has dropped since the 1990s, but the number of Category 4 and 5 hurricanes has nearly doubled over the past thirty-five years (averaging eighteen per year since 1990). New climate models out of NASA in 2007 show that the most violent and severe storms and tornadoes may become more common as our climate warms. So, what can we do?

Thinking Big

Some believe there are compelling arguments for both man-made and natural causes, but regardless of who or what is to blame, climate change is a major problem, affecting every single one of us. The most heartening news is that as a country and as a world we're finally *getting* it. Did you see the Live Earth concert? Two billion people watched that global concert event held on every continent! Ever hear the expression "Think globally, act locally"? That's exactly what a lot of governments are doing. All around the world people are banding together in international coalitions to study, report on, and combat the effects of global warming—and then people are taking action in their own backyards.

For example, the Intergovernmental Panel on Climate Change, or IPCC, is a coalition of experts who review the work of scientists researching global climate change (measuring the melting of glaciers, creating computer models projecting rising water levels, tracking the increased number of highly destructive storms, etc.). For the IPCC's most recent paper on the state of global warming, people from more than one hundred thirty countries, including more than twenty-five hundred expert reviewers and thirteen hundred authors, contributed. The IPCC shared the 2007 Nobel Peace Prize with Al Gore for their work on raising awareness of this threat.

There have been many other international efforts to find solutions. In 1997, the United Nations introduced the Kyoto Protocol with the objective that countries would work together to reduce greenhouse gases. Under the agreement, countries have to either commit to reducing these gas levels or do emissions trading to, in effect, pay for going above agreed-upon limits. As of June 2007, one hundred seventy parties had signed on to the Kyoto Protocol. (Sadly, the United States hasn't signed on.) Although the protocol involves commitments between 2008 and 2012, many countries began taking steps to reduce their emissions ahead of schedule.

These kinds of action-oriented international coalitions *have* worked before. For example, in 1987, before Tosh was even born, the Montreal Protocol was proposed as an international treaty designed to reduce depletion of the ozone layer. Eventually more than 191 nations signed on, pledging to reduce the use of substances such as chlorofluorocarbons. Jackpot! The depletion of the ozone layer has slowed down significantly in the last ten years—and most believe it's because so many countries successfully reduced their use of CFCs. The Montreal Protocol has been called one of the most successful international programs to date—and it shows what we can do when we put our heads together.

It's clear: Together, we're better. Here's another example: Under the guidance of the William J. Clinton Foundation, sixteen cities—Bangkok, Berlin, Chicago, Houston, Johannesburg, Karachi, London, Melbourne, Mexico City, Mumbai, New York, Rome, São Paulo, Seoul, Tokyo, and Toronto—have partnered with five major banks and dozens of companies and organizations to invest in ways to cut back on energy use in cities and to minimize greenhouse gas emissions. This Clinton Climate Initiative is making office buildings greener, ensure new construction causes fewer emissions, work with large companies to make energy-efficient products more affordable for consumers, and more.

There are hundreds, if not thousands, of international efforts to address global warming—and many reasons to feel hopeful that we'll be able to solve this problem.

Thinking Small

You have the power to make a difference with every choice you make, and that starts with the food you put into your mouth. As we'll discuss in the next chapter, lessening your intake of animal products could be your most important contribution. A United Nations report reveals that the world's rapidly growing herds of cattle (to feed expanding human populations) are the greatest threat to our climate, forests, and wildlife. In fact, livestock production takes up a whopping 30 percent of the land surface of the globe, and 70 percent of our increasingly precious agricultural land. Yikes. Veggie burgers, anyone?

While you're pondering that one, take a few moments to figure what your carbon footprint is—the amount of greenhouse gases you're personally cranking out into the atmosphere—so you know the impact your actions have on the earth. There are many ways to do this; we calculated ours in a few minutes through the Environmental Protection Agency at www.epa.gov/climatechange/emissions /ind_calculator.html. This website page asks you to plug in information about the temperature of your home, how far your family drives every week, whether you use energy-efficient appliances, and so on.

Next, you can move toward being carbon neutral. This means doing what you can to neutralize your use of the fossil fuels that pump all those harmful greenhouse gases into the atmosphere; the chapters ahead will give you dozens of suggestions that can help. But we live in a world where sometimes you've got to boot up your computer, order a burrito, or drive a car. So what can you do then? Your family might want to consider purchasing carbon offsets, alternative energy credits to offset your usage. For example, if a family of four decides to fly coast to coast, you can buy carbon offset credits that neutralize the effects of the greenhouse gases and energy expended for that flight. It's like you're subtracting what you put out into the atmosphere by purchasing credits for emission reduction gained elsewhere. Think of it like this: You're earning extra credit when you support wind farms, solar installations, or energy efficiency projects somewhere in the world. (It's not really "extra," because you can't erase your impact altogether, but it's more "extra" than not doing it. If the earth were your science teacher, we bet you'd earn a higher grade!) Go to www.fightglobalwarming.com to check out the carbon offset websites Environmental Defense recommends.

We can't resist telling you about one man's efforts to change the world, because it's such an inspiring example for us all. With all the focus on how to put less carbon dioxide into the atmosphere, we're fascinated by Richard Branson's interest in finding out how to remove the carbon dioxide that's already there. This British entrepreneur, the genius behind Virgin Records and Virgin airlines, has offered a $25 million prize to anyone who can combat global warming by coming up with a way to remove at least a billion tons of carbon dioxide from the atmosphere every year. Branson has roped in former Vice President Al Gore to be one of the judges for this Virgin Earth Challenge, which has leaders and innovators in the field scurrying to win the prize. One idea is to have a type of giant air filter perched on every building. Yup. Sounds good to us!

It may be years before scientists claim this prize. Maybe you'll be on the team of inventors! Sounds better than sitting around waiting to win the lottery, right?

dwindling fossil fuel reserves

Gas prices are headline news—*even* if you're not driving yet. It's hard to miss the news stories on the price of a gallon. Gas prices are soaring in part because all fossil fuels—including gasoline, oil, petroleum, and coal—are nonrenewable resources. It took the earth millions and millions of years to make them, but in barely a hundred and fifty years we've managed to burn through our reserves so quickly that we're in danger of running out altogether. We're facing hard choices if we keep relying on fossil fuels: greater dependence on foreign countries, where so many oil reserves lie, or the need to drill into protected land in the United States to get more oil, or dig up more coal, with all the risks that mining entails.

It's not just the gas for our cars and the oil to heat our homes we're worried about. Most of us can't go for long without eating or using a product that is somehow tied to the fossil fuel industry. Food, toiletries, toys, computers, homes—just about everything you can think of is derived from or stored in products made from the petroleum we get from oil—and of course we use it to power the trucks, ships, and planes that bring everything to us.

Our dwindling oil reserves offer perhaps the best example of how when one part of the green machine breaks down, it can stress the rest of the machine. Let's say we decide we don't want to use any more oil, so we'll just dig up more coal for energy. Now we've got to drill down deeper into coal mines, putting miners at risk. Or if that coal lies beneath a mountain, as it often does, we'll have to blow up the mountain and all the forests around it to get at that coal. And burning coal creates its own mess of pollutants, particularly greenhouse gases. China and India are building hundreds of coal plants because coal there is so plentiful and therefore cheap—but some scientists say that the increased carbon dioxide production from that coal will cancel out any benefits from the Kyoto agreement.

So how do we deal with the dwindling supplies of gas and oil and other fossil fuels without making global warming worse?

Thinking Big

Who says cars have to run on gas? They don't! As we'll talk about more in the "Green Wheels" chapter, there are cars powered by ethanol, hydrogen, electricity, or biodiesel—to name just a few alternatives—zipping along our highways right now. The race is on to find the best energy alternatives to fossil fuels, not only for running our cars, but for powering the rest of our lives as well.

Scientists all over the world are pouring their efforts into testing renewable energy sources—something the earth happily makes more of. For more and more countries the answer to improvements in electricity really is blowing in the wind—those cool three-bladed wind turbines are producing almost seventy-four billion watts' worth of electricity! Germany leads the world in wind power, but the United States installed 2,434 megawatts (at a cost of 4 billion dollars) in 2006, moving up to second place by 2007, with Spain coming in third.

Sunlight is another answer to our dwindling supply of fossil fuels. Did you know that the sunlight hitting the earth in sixty seconds has enough power to supply the entire planet with its energy needs for one year? The goal of the Solar America Initiative (a U.S. Department of Energy program) is to turn more of that light into usable energy. The technology for harnessing solar power through panels has been around for a while—you've probably seen those blue contraptions on roofs for years. But there's a new effort to convert more of that energy into electricity by using photovoltaic cells (using semiconductors to convert sunlight into electricity), by concentrating solar power (collecting sunlight to power generators), and by using solar light (channeling the sun's rays into fiberoptic light).

Thousands of people are working on innovations such as these (maybe you will too one day?), and the goal of the Solar America Initiative is to have solar energy competitive with every other source of electricity by 2015. Holla!

Thinking Small

Maybe Mom and Dad won't go for buying a hybrid car. That doesn't mean you can't do your part right now by becoming less dependent on fossil fuels. You can get a solar charger for your cell phone, MP3 player, or computer. Or start driving less and walking or biking more. Or carpooling instead of riding solo. The idea is to consume less. In the end sometimes the greenest choice isn't what you do; it's what you *don't* do. Your decision to not get into the car, to not drive to the mall, to not buy another *whatever* is as powerful a demonstration of your commitment to reducing your reliance on fossil fuels as installing that solar panel on the garage.

worldwide water shortages

Consider this: All of the water presently in the world is the exact same water that was here millions of years ago! Our planet is so perfectly protected and recycles its water so efficiently that it stays within the system rather than drifting out into space. When you brush your teeth tonight, you could be using molecules of water a dinosaur literally bathed in!

Where it gets tricky, though, is that nearly all of the water on earth isn't fit for human consumption. Not even dinosaurs could stomach it. Most of the water on the planet—97 percent of it—is in the oceans: too salty to drink unless we treat it.

Since most of the world's water is saline—great for contact lenses, bad for people—that leaves only 3 percent in freshwater form. Of that, most of it—about 69 percent—is frozen in glaciers and ice caps, primarily in Antarctica and Greenland. People often think the rest is in rivers and lakes. True, that's where most of the water you use comes from (for example, the Colorado River supplies 60 percent of the water for Southern California), but it's only a very small percentage of the world's freshwater, about 0.3 percent. And lakes are vanishing—thousands around the world have already disappeared or are nearly gone.

Three countries—Chad, Niger, and Nigeria—depend on water from Lake Chad in Africa. This once-huge lake was at 5 percent of its capacity at the end of 2007, with more and more mouths desperate for what was left. All over the world, river and stream water is being diverted for the irrigation of crops to feed increasing populations (more than 90 percent of the growth of the human population has occurred in recent decades). That redistribution of water is further shrinking lakes already burdened by drought and higher temperatures.

So where does most of our freshwater come from? It's found deep underground as groundwater after rain, snow, and melting ice have percolated down. To get the water from these aquifers means we've got to pump it up from far below the earth's surface, which takes a lot of oil. And the job gets harder every day because more than half of the world's population live in places where the water tables—the portion of ground beneath the earth that is saturated with water—are getting lower. Drought and overpopulation are major culprits. Drought is a growing worldwide problem—and it's in our backyard, too. By May of 2007, 24 percent of the continental United States reported severe to extreme drought. If there's no rain, it makes sense that nothing's replenishing the aquifers.

If our numbers keep growing at the same rate, there will be 7.5 billion people on Earth by 2020 and 9 billion people by 2050. All those people mean that we've got to pump more water out of the ground, which just lowers the water tables even more. And not all aquifers can be replenished; if we pump too much, the wells can go dry—which is happening now, even in the United States. Thousands of farms in Texas, Oklahoma, and Kansas have simply run out of water, which has had a huge effect on the grain harvest. Some scientists say that by 2025 two-thirds of humans won't have safe water to drink or wash with. That's major. We've got one thirsty green machine.

Thinking Big

We wish we could report more progress in the efforts to fight the growing problem of water shortages. True, countries across the globe are building desalination plants, which filter out the salt from ocean water so it becomes drinkable. However, these plants are expensive to build and operate, and of course they've got to spend loads of energy to carry the purified water over long distances. They also leave behind massive salt deposits, which are tricky to dispose of because we don't want the salt to trickle back into groundwater or, if left in the oceans, to risk harming marine life. It seems that just as people argued for a long time over whether global warming was a real threat and something we needed to take immediate action on, the world has been slow to recognize that we've got to get serious about saving our water supply. Probably the best news to report is that internationally, concerned groups such as the World Health Organization and the United Nations are working hard to bring our attention to the immediacy of the problem so we understand that the water shortage is everyone's concern.

Thinking Small

Once you're aware of the growing scarcity of our most precious resource, it's easy to spot all the ways we just let water run down the drain. Tosh grew up watching his parents catch rainwater off the roof in huge underground cisterns, which was then used in the garden. More recently his father installed inexpensive filters so that rainwater could be used in showers, in toilets, and for dish washing. If, like Tosh, you want to collect rainwater for your garden, all you have to do to start is buy a plastic trash can to place under your rain gutter.

You can also look at the way you drink water. Obviously, you'll want to think about wasting less of it. But also make the connection between two different parts of the green machine: the water you drink and the energy it took to bring it to your door. You probably don't remember it, but ten years ago we weren't all running around clutching disposable water bottles or stashing cases of them in our homes. Empty plastic bottles weren't spilling out of the trash cans at your school, or piling up around the track or football field. Grocery store aisles weren't stacked to the ceilings with different brands of water, with advertisers working hard to convince us the water from our own taps wasn't good enough. Stop and think about how much energy it took to pump that water out of the ground, to manufacture the bottles to contain it, and then to ship it—sometimes halfway around the world. If the water in your home doesn't taste good or you worry about contaminants, there are plenty of ways to filter it inexpensively. You can very affordably mount a filter right on your faucet or under the sink. (Our friend has a faucet filter that provides the same amount of water as if she'd bought seven hundred fifty plastic bottles, at only ten cents per gallon!) If you need to carry water with you, invest in a reusable water bottle. And if you're going to buy bottled water, check the packaging and choose the bottle made with the least plastic—some weigh 30 to 40 percent less. Read the label and go for the brand that's made the closest to where you live—that means it took less petroleum to ship it to your store.

losing our topsoil and trees

The top few inches of soil all over the earth are called topsoil. This thin layer took millions of years to accumulate. Trees and plants grow in it, and these, in turn, keep the soil from blowing away. When the vegetation that holds everything in place disappears—because of overgrazing of cattle, overfarming, drought, or fire—the land becomes incredibly vulnerable, especially to mud slides after heavy rains.

Remember *The Grapes of Wrath*? Those migrant Okies were farmers and crop-pickers driven West when overgrazing, overfarming, and drought destroyed the topsoil. Farms turned into acres upon acres of dust overnight. You've seen pictures of the 1930s Dust Bowl on the Great Plains in your textbooks. Remember the massive black clouds overtaking cars, people, and whole farms? Similar volatile dust storms are occurring today and can be seen in satellite images over China and Africa.

Deforestation—the deliberate cutting down of trees to be used as lumber for buildings, pulp for paper, or fuel for burning—is another related international crisis. You've probably heard about how the tropical rain forests, which are home to an astonishingly high percentage of plant and animal species, are rapidly disappearing. But until the space age gave us satellite imagery in the 1960s, we had no idea how fast the rain forests were being destroyed. Until then, scientists relied on photos taken from weather balloons and airplanes to monitor earth changes, but satellite tracking convinced many experts that between 1960 and 1990, humans had destroyed a third of the planet's rain forests—along with more plants and animals than you can imagine. Some satellites, like Landsat and SAR, have a 92 percent accuracy rate, and as scientists studied that data, they realized that the rain forest was vanishing twice as fast as they'd thought, with 25 percent more carbon dioxide being released. At this rate there'll be no more rain forests by 2090. In developing countries in South America, Asia, and Africa, the loss of forests to clear-cutting and burning is dramatic. Since 1990 we've lost about thirteen million hectares a year, or an area the size of Kansas. And we have the same problem close to home too. In the United States researchers are guessing that we'll lose another twenty-three million acres of forestland by 2050. Again, one part of the green machine's breaking down grinds another part to a halt: Cutting down the forests, which produce oxygen and consume carbon dioxide, not only leaves more carbon dioxide in the air, but also depletes water from the soil and inhibits the amount of water that can replenish aquifers or add moisture to the atmosphere.

> You've heard of the great Mayan civilization, but do you know why they disappeared? It's now believed that these advanced farmers may have contributed to their own demise by deforesting their lands too quickly, eroding the soil, and creating a fatal food shortage—a lesson our own civilization might do well to heed!

Thinking Big

Can this process be stopped? Hey, we did it before. In 1935, FDR began the Soil Conservation Service, which helped restore ecological balance by, among other things, planting millions of trees to reduce the dust by 60 percent. More recently, according to UNICEF, we're doing enough replanting, reforesting, and landscape restoration worldwide to reduce the twenty-three million acre net loss to 7.3 million acres per year (or the size of Panama, which is an improvement). Further from home, Dr. Wangari Maathai, the first African woman to receive the Nobel Peace Prize for what the Nobel Committee called her "contribution to sustainable development, democracy, and peace," founded the Green Belt Movement in 2004, which has been responsible for planting more than thirty million trees in Kenya to help restore topsoil. No wonder they call her the "Tree Mother of Africa"!

South Korea deserves a high five for cluing in to the growing problem of deforestation in that country forty-five years ago, when at the end of the Korean War people realized that almost all the trees had been cut down and burned for fuel. President Park Chung Hee launched a huge reforestation project, mobilizing villages to join together as cooperatives. The result? Nothing short of astonishing! Hundreds of thousands of South Koreans went out, dug trenches, and planted trees. Today more than 65 percent of South Korea is covered in lush green forests again!

Thinking Small

There's a lot you can do on a small scale, such as plant trees or contribute to charities that do the planting for you. Linda has a friend who rescues the plants and trees dug up by construction workers that are destined to be thrown away; she then plants them in her own yard or finds new homes for them. A lot of youth group members gain community service credits by planting local gardens. If your community doesn't have a Christmas tree recycling program, perhaps you could look into starting one. On the home front, you can also press your internal pause button before you press the print button. Do you really need to print out that copy? And can you recycle the paper before it even hits the bin? Use the back of sheets for future printing or for scratch paper, for example.

desertification

Imagine living on a rural farm near a desert and watching your land and home becoming covered by sand. That desertification is an all-too real experience for hundreds of thousands of people who've watched their entire villages overrun by encroaching deserts in places such as China and Africa. In fact, the Gobi Desert is expanding by nine hundred fifty square miles per year and is now only one hundred fifty miles from Beijing, a city of fifteen million. Desertification happens because people have cut down too many trees (which held water in the soil) and have overgrazed cattle, and because drought has killed off too much vegetation.

Desertification is affecting almost every continent. Ghana and Nigeria struggle with the problem. Afghanistan, Kazakhstan, Kyrgyzstan, Tajikistan, Turkmenistan, and Uzbekistan are threatened by encroaching deserts. Madagascar has already lost about 10 percent of its land to desert. Mexico and Brazil are also under threat. This problem even affects the United States: Overgrazing has caused sand dunes to form near Freeport, Maine, in the Rio Puerco Basin of New Mexico, and elsewhere in the Southwest.

Desertification doesn't merely threaten the production of crops for humans and livestock; the Sahelian drought and desertification that began four decades ago in Africa was responsible for the deaths of up to a quarter of a million people and the loss of agriculture in five countries. Desertification also jeopardizes biodiversity by destroying fragile ecosystems. Looming sand dunes are as vulnerable to destructive avalanches as snow dunes are.

Thinking Big

But people are thinking outside of the sandbox. For example, scientists from the Chinese government's Ministry of Forestry have started building the Great Green Wall of China—twenty-eight thousand miles of forest designed to halt the advance of the desert. By 2010, they hope to have planted more than nine million acres of trees and low-lying support vegetation. In the Middle East, farmers are building sand fences to stabilize sand dunes the way Americans use snow fences to keep snow from piling up in huge drifts.

Thinking Small

In addition to donating to organizations that help in the restoration effort by providing tree seedlings and instructions for their planting and care, you might want to pledge money to organizations that provide people with solar ovens. A lot of deforestation happens when native people cut down wood for heating homes and for cooking food. Solar ovens give them the chance to use a more readily available resource, which allows the local vegetation to regrow and hold off the advancement of the desert.

the collapse of ocean ecosystems

The oceans of the world may have different names—the Pacific, Atlantic, Indian, Arctic, and Southern—but a quick peek at a map reveals that they're all connected. There's just one massive body of water flowing around different landmasses that were once connected as well. Our point? If you dump something in one ocean, it affects the others. So when you hear that cruise ships, for example, are allowed to release treated sewage while at sea (for a large vessel, that could be upward of thirty thousand gallons of human waste a day), and then you stop to think about the billions of people who live near the world's oceans (and pollute that water through public waste streams), you can see how we're literally turning our seas into sewers. (If you read Carl Hiaasen's *Flush,* you might remember that Noah's dad was so angry at the local casino boat for dumping raw sewage that he sank it—not a solution we'd recommend for you!)

In Linda's environmental engineering course at the University of Southern California years ago, her textbook warned that the world's oceans could be dead within fifty years. Many scientists believe we're right on course, if not ahead of schedule. More of our world's oceans are developing dead zones—areas where there's virtually no dissolved oxygen in the water, meaning that fish, zooplankton, crabs, shrimp, and any other life forms can't survive—which also threatens those of us who depend on them for sustenance. These dead zones are mostly in Europe and on the East Coast of the United States and range from less than a mile to forty-five thousand square miles. The UN Environment Programme (UNEP) says that the number of these dead zones may have increased by a third in just two years—to around two hundred. What's causing them? Pollution from human and animal waste, the burning of fossil fuels, and the dumping of and runoff from fertilizers, which deprive the water of oxygen and create large spreading masses, or blooms, of small plants called phytoplankton. These blooms are growing out of control and depleting the water of even more oxygen.

Huge waste dumps of plastic are also leading to the destruction of ocean ecosystems. Plastics dumped into the ocean become feeding grounds for fish, which swallow them and choke or strangle to death. Fish populations are also threatened by overfishing; 90 percent of the big fish—including several species of tuna, marlin, swordfish, and shark—are now gone, with other species teetering on the brink. To a certain extent we're victims of our own success; the technology for catching greater numbers of fish has improved so rapidly that we're scooping up larger catches than ever, which doesn't give the remaining fish enough time to repopulate. According to the Food and Agriculture Organization of the United Nations, fully 75 percent of all fish have been overfished or depleted.

What few people understand is that the oxygen we breathe comes more from the ocean than from the world's forests—as much as 70 to 80 percent! (Most of it comes from the atmosphere or is produced by phytoplankton.) There's no way to underscore the importance of cleaning up our oceans and helping fish populations rebound.

Thinking Big

Since our oceans are connected and affect every continent on Earth, doesn't it make sense that we should get connected too to protect them? International organizations such as the Western and Central Pacific Fisheries Commission are imposing quotas and moratoriums on catching fish vulnerable to extinction, in the hope that these populations can recover. Following the example of Point Lobos State Reserve, a seven-hundred-fifty-acre marine reserve off the coast of Southern California, governments are looking to establish protective marine parks the same way we've sheltered our land with parks and wilderness reserves. In the United States, organizations such as the Natural Resources Defense Council are urging the government to tighten up regulations on sewage dumping, control development that can threaten fragile ecosystems, and prevent farms and factories from putting more pollution into coastal waters. And speaking of connection, every step we take to control global warming helps damp down the phytoplankton blooms that starve our oceans of oxygen.

Thinking Small

Go to www.foodandwaterwatch.org and download their online Smart Seafood Guide to find out which fish are safe to eat without doing too much harm to remaining populations. If you live within a short driving distance to an ocean, river, stream, or lake, organize a school field trip and launch a Clean Up the Water trash collection day at your school. Of course you can also hold a school fundraiser for your favorite ocean charity and help them do the work by funding their efforts. And you might want to think about convincing your parents to treat your lawn organically instead of using the commonly used nitrogen-rich fertilizer that's a big source of the dead-zone problem.

electropollution

One hundred years ago much less electricity was in the air. Now our green machine is getting zapped more or less constantly. Think about all the relatively recent inventions you use every day that require electricity—your phone, iPod, TV, hair straightener, computer, stereo, lights, microwave, and other appliances. All that electricity flying around the air generates electromagnetic fields, or EMFs. The EMFs are especially strong near transformers, power lines, cell phone towers, and other locations that create or rout electricity. Scientists have been studying the safety of EMFs for years. There have been some worrying reports that high levels of EMFs might be responsible for causing certain types of cancers. Some teens and their parents are wondering if that might pose a health concern, considering all the hours we're pressing those cell phones to our ears or running around with them in our pockets. Other studies say we don't have enough evidence to make the link. What most scientists agree on is that, given the growth of EMFs, we need to do a lot more research so we can be sure that electropollution isn't jeopardizing our health.

Thinking Big

One of the reasons it's difficult to figure out whether EMFs pose a health risk is that scientists get their best information from long-term studies involving a great number of people, and many of the technologies we rely on today haven't been around for all that long. Think of how much more time people spend in front of their computers or on PDAs and cell phones than they did six or eight years ago. We definitely need studies that reflect the changing ways we use products that generate EMFs. That's why in 1996 the World Health Organization (WHO) started the International EMF Project. It set out to study the best available research, figure out where we needed to gather more data, report on any health risks, and create international standards so we could minimize those risks. The WHO is scheduled to release its final report in 2008. This is another example of how making sure our earth is healthy helps keep us healthy. Pooling our brainpower around the world will help us figure out how to respond to increasing EMF levels.

Thinking Small

You don't have to wait until studies are definitive to take some simple precautions. Just remember that the farther away from the source of EMFs, the less exposure you have to them. So try to sit an arm's length away from your computer. Walk across the room from your microwave while you're heating your lasagna. Stick your alarm clock across the room.

(Think how much more awake you'll be when you have to get out of bed to turn it off!) Stash your cell phone in your locker or at least your backpack when it's on but you're not using it, instead of in your pocket. When you're using it, try putting it on speaker or plugging into a headset. Then, at home, switch to a landline—remember those phones with actual cords? When using a cordless, try a headset as well, since batteries also generate EMFs. At least some of the time try letting your hair air-dry instead of using a hair dryer, and use a regular razor (preferably one of the new recycled plastic ones with removable heads) instead of an electric one.

WHERE ARE ALL THE BUZZING BEES?

"Remember strawberries, peaches, and almonds?" That's what you might be saying soon if hives of fifty thousand honeybees keep vanishing overnight worldwide, their beekeepers finding hives devastated. This is called Colony Collapse Disorder (CCD), and no one knows the cause for sure. Some blame mites and parasites, or pesticides that weaken bees' immune systems, causing them to lose their sense of direction. Others say that genetically engineered crops, or maybe cell phones, are to blame. Expert Marla Spivak told *60 Minutes* that bees reflect our own stress. "They're giving us feedback. Their environment is not healthy, and they're saying, 'I can't live here. It's toxic.'"

growing landfills, shrinking land

Think about everything you've thrown away—just in the last twenty-four hours. We sort our recyclables from the trash and roll it all out to the curb, where the big trucks haul it away every week. And next week we have more where that came from. Let's think about this for a second: Ever wonder about where they're going with your junk, and how far they have to drive to get it there? Is it true that these holes in the ground—landfills—are filling up? And that the poisons from these landfills are leaking into our groundwater?

Sure, no one wants a smelly landfill in his or her backyard, but it's gotta be in someone's backyard, right? Problem is, we're running out of backyards! According to the Environmental Protection Agency, there will be room available for only 1,234 landfills in the United States in 2008—that's about eighteen thousand fewer than were available in 1978—and these landfills are getting bigger, taking up more and more space. And unfortunately, landfills do leach toxins into the groundwater, because the clay and plastic liners—some only a tenth of an inch thick—haven't turned out to be impervious to leakage. Sometimes water trickles through the landfills and absorbs the toxins, which make their way through the soil or are pumped into nearby ponds. Contaminants can be released into the air when waste is crushed or burned.

Thinking Big

People are finally wising up to the idea that we shouldn't just dump everything into landfills, which is lessening our need for them. But we have a long way to go. Between 40 and 50 percent of landfills consist of paper products, many of which could have been recycled. Disposable diapers are the third largest consumer item in landfills, a fact to consider the next time you babysit. All over America there are programs for safe disposal of computers, paint, batteries, cell phones (which are filled with arsenic, lead, and mercury), and the like—and programs for more education about how to recycle our larger durable goods so they don't make landfills continue to swell.

However, as long as we're stuck with landfills, waste management experts are figuring out how to take the landfill gases (LFG) and turn them into useful energy. Harnessing these LFGs actually puts less methane into the air, which means less global warming. This is the kind of trash talk we love!

Thinking Small

We wouldn't have to worry so much about our landfills if we were more careful about what we toss away. Instead of pitching your old computer, take it in to be reconditioned and have the hard drive wiped. Then donate it to a school or shelter. Patronize stores that reward customers for recycling—the local coffee shop that gives free refills to customers who bring in their own travel mugs, or the beauty product manufacturer that gives you a discount if you bring in your old jar for a fresh dollop of moisturizer. It feels good not to be part of the throw-away culture.

small voice, big issue:
AN INTERVIEW WITH SAMANTHA LITCHFORD

We hope this chapter has demonstrated that a single action matters. For fourteen-year-old Samantha Litchford of Rustburg, Virginia, it all began with hearing about a major problem in the green machine, learning how world leaders were thinking big about solutions, then thinking small by taking up the challenge of having her voice heard.

"Low pressure system," "climate peak," "meteorology"—these are now everyday terms for Samantha. It started when she saw a video about tornadoes at age seven. "Of course I fell in love with it," she says matter-of-factly. "And then I fell in love with meteorology and realized that this is what I want to do." A few years later, she watched in horror as the film *The Day After Tomorrow* depicted the catastrophes and disasters that could happen if global warming continues. "It was just sci-fi, but scary—huge low pressure systems tearing up everything, tornadoes in California, New York flooding and freezing." And while she knows the movie exaggerates, she thinks its message of urgency is true. "I was, like, 'This could really happen.'"

But what could a kid do? Well, first, get educated. She did research online and watched the Discovery Channel to learn as much as possible. "And of course I fell in love with climatology," she says. But the more she learned, the more concerned she became. If the polar ice caps melt, "it could wipe out species of animals. There would be global starvation, and basically the extinction of the human race. And I thought, 'This could happen in my lifetime—or my kid's lifetime. Something needs to be done.'" But few people shared her alarm.

Then she saw an ad that read: "Journalist wanted" in

Studio2B, her local Girl Scout council magazine. "I always knew I could write," says Samantha, a cadette scout. Her article about climate change got so much attention that she was selected to attend the sixtieth annual UN DPI/NGO Conference in September of 2007, Climate Change: How It Impacts Us All. There were speakers from around the world, and the three-day conference really woke her up to the scope of the problem and how many indigenous people could be devastated by climate change. "That was hurtful and horrible to hear," she says.

Samantha knows her mission in life is to wake people up to the eco-disasters that loom in the future if we don't act now. "My friends are still on the borderline of believing or not believing me," she says, but perhaps one day she'll change their minds when she gets a Ph.D. in meteorology and/or climatology. Right now she's focused on getting the word out through her writing. Her dream? "To be a full-time activist, write books, and work for the Weather Channel."

a handy guide for thinking ahead:
THE FIVE Rs

Now you've got the lowdown on the most important environmental issues. We hope they feel more real to you, that you're starting to have a sense that these problems aren't "out there" somewhere. They have real effects on our world, right now. And so can you. The upcoming chapters will help you see how what you do every day can affect these huge problems of global warming, water shortages, and so on. We'll give you lots of ideas about how you can take individual action to lessen your impact on the environment. As we said in the introduction, every day is an opportunity to start fresh, to make a new set of decisions about what small step you can take to live greener.

There's a really handy way you can figure out how to think small and think green. Follow the five Rs: reduce, reuse, recycle, rethink, refuse. Use these five terms to help guide your thinking about any decision, and know that one small act, combined with the small acts of millions of other committed individuals like yourself, will have a giant impact.

You've seen the triangular logo with the three arrows chasing each other. Let's review those familiar three Rs:

REDUCE: Take a pause and ask yourself, "Could I make do with less of this?" Less water in my shower? Less shampoo on my head? Then turn the question sideways: Of course some packaging can be important to protect a certain product. But do I want to support a company that dresses up its product with a ton of flashy extra packaging (ever open a huge box to find the contents squished into one lonely corner?) when I could give my money to a company that packages an equally great product in a much more efficient way, perhaps even from recycled materials?

REUSE: Before you throw anything away, could you use it again, or use it for a different purpose? If you're going to buy a beverage in a plastic bottle, could you minimize its impact by refilling that bottle a few times?

RECYCLE: We know all about recycling paper, plastic, and glass, but can you also consider recycling . . . books? Clothes? Old CDs? How can you look at what you have and figure out how to re-purpose it? How can you find someone who needs your old bike, Mac laptop, video game?

Now we'd like you to add two more Rs to the familiar trio.

Our friend David de Rothschild is heir to one of the most famous banking fortunes in the world. But instead of living a life of leisure, David's busy trekking the globe reporting on environmental crises and the effects of global warming. His educational foundation, Adventure Ecology, has inspired us to include this fourth R:

RETHINK: Advertisers spend billions telling you their latest gizmo will make you happy. If we don't stop to think it through, we might find ourselves automatically buying things we don't really want or need. Start by asking yourself if you really need to upgrade your phone just yet. Do you really want to buy the latest iPod when your two-year-old version still works? Or the flattest screen TV that requires special DVDs? You certainly don't need to lead a life of total self-denial, but it can help to think before every purchase to make sure you're buying it for reasons you feel good about.

With gratitude, we borrow our fifth R from Eustace Conway, a naturalist and the founder of the Turtle Island Preserve in North Carolina. When he was only twelve, Eustace lived in the woods for a week. At seventeen he left his parents' home to live in a tepee in the forest and caught his food with his bare hands! Conway now spends his life teaching people how to live more simply, authentically, and naturally. He suggests you also:

REFUSE: When you decide *not* to buy something and decide to find a new, different way to use what you've got, you might find that you stretch your mind in all sorts of creative ways. Necessity is the mother of invention, right? What happens when you decide not to buy the latest CD or DVD or video game or Abercrombie shirt or UGG boots or . . . or . . . or . . . ?

It's really interesting to see the different ways you can define yourself when you don't let your possessions define you. What can your life become when you stop depending so much on stuff?

Five fingers. Five Rs. Coincidence? We think not. Make it second nature. When you're not sure whether to do something, tick through your fingers and quickly run down the list—reduce, reuse, recycle, rethink, refuse—and see if any of them could apply. The result? A greener choice. A greener world.

And keep in mind: It's not always what you do that has the biggest impact, but often what you don't do—to your mother, that is.

EATING GREEN

T he very day **we started** writing this book, we **got into** a mother-son argument over junk food. The episode went something like this:

Tosh (to himself): Omg. It's a miracle! There's *actually* a soda in our fridge. There's *never* soda in our fridge. I have no clue how it got there—Mom's friend must have left it? I better chug it now because I've got about thirty seconds before she realizes I'm awake and checks to see that I'm eating a "healthy" breakfast.

Linda walks in as Tosh lifts the can to his lips.

Linda: Is that soda? How could you put that into your body first thing in the morning?

Linda pulls the can out of Tosh's hand.

Tosh: Come on, Mom! It's from Whole Foods, anyway.

Linda scans the label.

Linda: Yeah, but look at these ingredients. I hear it takes thirty-two glasses of water to neutralize the acid in one can of soda? And it was shipped all the way from

New Jersey. Do you realize how much gas a truck had to use to get this can to California?

Tosh: Mom, please. Can't I just be a normal teenager today? Jake's mom doesn't freak if he has a can of soda in the morning.

Linda arches an eyebrow. Tosh sighs and sets the can of soda down.

Tosh: Okay, Mom, you win. Where's the OJ?

Maybe someone in your family reminds you of Tosh's mom—always looking over your shoulder to make sure you eat your veggies and stay clear of too much junk food. If so, be grateful that someone around you knows how important healthy eating is for you. Years ago Linda met a beautiful woman in her seventies who looked fifty—tops (and that was without plastic surgery!). Encouraged, Linda asked the woman what her secret was.

"Oh, that's easy," she replied. "I eat mostly organic raw fruits and vegetables. Try it! For years you may not notice much of a difference, but stick with them. The older you get, the more people will notice that you look and act so much younger than you are! It's as if all the living cells in the food give you added beauty and energy other people my age can't access."

when did natural food become unnatural?

It's only very recently in our history that people stopped eating natural unprocessed foods. According to *Plenty* magazine, fifteen thousand new food products are introduced each year in our country, and 75 percent of those are heavily processed candies, condiments, breakfast cereals, baked goods, beverages, or dairy novelties!

How did this happen? Why did we stop eating wholesome, natural foods and instead start depending so heavily on grains stripped of most of their nutrients, meat from animals pumped up with hormones and antibiotics, fruits and vegetables with the vitamins boiled right out of them and canned with tons of sodium and preservatives, and junk food filled with empty calories from sugar—all washed down with soda and coffee that gets us jittery from all that caffeine?

Let's start by going back to nature and seeing how food once grew without our interference; hindsight offers us valuable lessons. We'll then take a look at how much of our food is grown, shipped, processed, and preserved and see if we can make different choices to protect our health and our priceless natural ecosystems.

Have you spent long *quiet* hours in wild places? Probably not. Most of us live in cities and haven't been exposed to the natural world for long stretches. That doesn't mean we're totally disconnected, though. We know, for example, that the food waiting for us on supermarket shelves, in convenience stores, and in restaurants came from farms initially.

But where did food come from *before* farms? And before that? What was living and eating and breeding before our arrival on the planet?

the circle of life really is a circle

Obviously, wild plants and animals have flourished for millions of years on our planet without any help from humans. They've done this by being very connected to and dependent upon one another. For example, consider the millions upon millions of buffalo that used to freely roam the plains of North America—all grazing on wild grasses, spreading seeds and "fertilizer," and then poking the seeds into the soil with their hooves, literally eating and replanting the plains as they grazed. As leaves, branches, flowers, and seeds from all this vegetation died, they dropped to the ground, where their nutrients decomposed and were released back into the soil.

At the same time, millions upon millions of salmon swam freely from the oceans up the rivers of North America without any dams or industrial pollutants in their pathways. During their migrations, bears, eagles, wolves, and other predators would grab the salmon out of the water, chomping down the choicest cuts of fish and leaving the carcasses all over to decompose into natural fertilizer. That's how all the rich minerals and nutrients from the ocean were passed through the fish to the bears and then into the ground to fertilize plants.

The wind and rain blew and washed nutrients all over the world every day, soaking their nutrients deep into the soil and around the plant roots, where they were absorbed. Insects and microbes likewise did their part to spread nutrients through digestion and excretion.

This never-ending process is how millions of species

have thrived, sharing and spreading nutrients in this huge jigsaw puzzle of life, ensuring a dynamic equilibrium. This circle of life depending on other life is what E. O. Wilson first called biodiversity. It all operates on a handshake agreement between all life and all death, a combination that ensures eternal life.

where are humans in this circle?

But wait a minute. The world doesn't look like this anymore. Animals rarely interact in this way. And while humans used to harvest food from the wilds—often traveling nomadically with the fruit trees—things have changed a bit, haven't they? We've hunted a lot of species into extinction or near extinction. We've dammed rivers and ravaged the land, crowding out the native species. Our farming practices often leach the soil of nutrients rather than replenish them, and when we die, our bodies are encased in coffins, our ashes placed in urns, so that our nutrients can't return to the earth.

The medicine man in New Mexico used to share stories with us about what an honor it was for his elders to return to the earth, to the "Mother" to become part of the "full hoop" of life. His people were buried directly in the dirt, their bodies giving up nourishment to the one who had nourished them through so many winters. What a different mind-set from what we're raised with today!

That's not to say that human beings are no longer part of the circle of life—we're still made of flesh and bone—but most of us have fled the wisdom, stability, and sustainability of the family farm for the industrialized cities, where our cell phones, polyester clothes, cars, and video games couldn't be farther from nature. And most who *have* stayed behind on the farms are changing farming practices to meet the demands of convenience, overconsumption, and a taste for junk food that have nothing to do with truly nourishing ourselves and replenishing the circle of life.

industrial compared to organic farming

When the first Europeans arrived in the New World of America, they found an abundant land with wide open plains and lush, fertile farmland. People came in droves, racing across the land in covered wagons to claim their plots and clear and till the land and start their lives. Being a farmer and a rancher was the dream of millions, and towns and rural communities sprung up everywhere, creating a patchwork quilt of small town America that country songs still romanticize. The more fertile the land, the stronger the community. Everything—the success of the shops, churches, schools, doctor's offices, and restaurants—started with the health and productivity of the land.

But a growing economy during the industrial revolution demanded that a flood of the workforce leave the land to work in factories, while better technology and equipment allowed farmers to employ fewer people and reap larger harvests. Bit by bit, people left small towns for cities, which became a trend as the youth too were drawn to find their fortune—and excitement!—elsewhere. Communities began to lose their most vibrant members. Farmers became more dependent on improved farming technology when they saw that they could produce higher volumes of crops at reduced costs, and many smaller players couldn't adapt quickly enough so they lost their farms. Millions of Americans were ripped apart from their homes and farms—their heritage.

Today, only 2 percent of Americans are farmers, when one hundred years ago that number was 40 percent! If you go back to our nation's birth, the numbers were even more staggering. According to *Time* magazine, nine in ten citizens were farmers; now only one in one hundred fifty is. Whereas a hundred years ago most food was grown on small, local farms, nowadays much of our food is grown on huge industrial-size farms that resemble airports more than those storybook scenes with the big red barns. A century ago most farmers grew a variety of crops, rotating them so that the nutrients enhanced by the diverse crops would keep the ecology of the soil at its healthiest. Today's farmers grow mono-cropped commodities—usually only one crop, such as corn, cotton, or soybeans growing from one edge of a huge field to the other—because that's how farmers can benefit the most economically. The problem with a mono-crop is that if a disease to which the crop is vulnerable strikes, the disease will jump from one plant to another with no other variety of crops to slow it down. Entire crops can be destroyed in weeks or even days.

A pet project of Adolph Hitler's during WWII was the development of poisonous neurotoxins, or nerve gas. After the war several scientists figured out how to use an offshoot of this poison on plants as a pesticide. The World Health Organization estimates that pesticide poisoning kills twenty thousand people worldwide every year.

Without a diverse mix of plants able to resist a variety of diseases, the farmer must turn to the chemicals in fertilizers and pesticides to do the work that nature would normally have done. And unfortunately, those chemicals don't stay in one place or affect only the target pest. With wind and rain, chemicals drift far past the edges of fields where they're sprayed. Runoff from pesticides finds its way into streams, lakes, and oceans with rain and irrigation. Some chemicals percolate through the soil and into underground aquifers. Some farm chemicals are long-lasting and build up in the bodies of animals and humans. Some herbicides such as atrazine affect the embryonic development of frogs. Some soil fumigants eat away at the earth's ozone layer. Today's industrial farms are exactly the opposite of a healthy and diverse ecology.

Writer John E. Ikerd of the University of Missouri says that as we've specialized, standardized, and centralized control of agriculture to make it more efficient, we've forced living systems, including people, to behave as lifeless machines. He writes that as we've removed the

life from agriculture, we've also removed its soul. And
restoring life to rural communities can come about only by
restoring the life and health of agriculture, reclaiming the
sacred of food and farming.

back to basics: organic farming

Concern over the use of harmful chemicals and the desire
to restore the soul to agriculture are fueling the rise in
organic farming. Organic farming means raising crops
without synthetic fertilizers, pesticides, or plant growth
regulators. It relies on the modern application of some
time-honored technologies. For example, a certified
organic farmer uses natural nutrients including animal
manure, rotates and mixes crops to reduce diseases and
pests, interplants wild species to encourage pollinators
such as birds and beneficial insects, smothers weeds with
mulches (chipped branches, leaves, straw) to reduce or
eliminate the need for herbicides, and carefully observes
and mimics natural ecosystems in many other ways.

While the organic farming movement began as early
as the 1930s, it really began to take hold in the 1980s as
more environmentally aware consumers began to demand
healthier options. Over the last two decades, organic
farmers have become more sophisticated about the need
to consolidate distribution of organic goods so that this
food, which is more expensive to produce, becomes more
affordable.

The promise of organic farming is that as people go
back to simpler farming methods, the connection with

the land and surrounding communities will return. And
no one can deny that you get healthier, better-tasting
produce! Equally important is that organic crops are
less vulnerable to disease. Instead of planting, say, an
entire field of soybeans, an organic farmer might mix in
berries alternating with beans, herbs, onions, marigolds,
or squash. If insects carrying a disease to which soybeans
are vulnerable land in that field, they won't simply be able
to move from one soybean plant to the next, spreading
the disease as they go. They'll have to spend a lot of time
and energy walking, crawling, or flying to get to their
next meal . . . slowing down the rate of the spread of the
disease, during which the insects themselves can die off,
which spares the plants. Diversity protects plants. Organic
farmers also rotate their crops so that they'll contribute
different nutrients to the soil, which will then strengthen
the next diverse crop and lessen topsoil depletion.

Organic food sales are growing every year—a
good sign that more and more people understand the
importance of protecting their bodies and wild spaces by
using safer farming techniques. Again, it's nothing new. It's
our heritage.

how tosh and linda eat

Tosh is no stranger to homegrown organic produce,
often picking organic lettuce, herbs, tomatoes, peppers,
cucumbers, sunflower seeds, and fruit out of his garden.
Sometimes he whines about being asked to water in the
summer, but mostly he's a good sport because he loves

the fresher taste and because he's proud of eating what he's grown. When we buy organic produce (which is 99 percent of the time), we expect it to cost more because it's more expensive to grow. It's an investment in our health and in the earth—and one we're happy to make. Plus, we're fairly certain we can credit all the pure water and organic fruits and veggies Tosh eats for how little acne he's had as a teen.

Linda's mom was a health food enthusiast before it was mainstream, sending Linda to school with whole wheat veggie sandwiches that were so grainy they looked like her backyard mud pies (and were about as heavy, too!). Thankfully times have changed. Linda's a lifelong student in this arena, trying about every variation of healthy eating you can imagine—including phases that were pretty "out there." She was a "fruitarian" when she was pregnant with Tosh and stuck to a diet of organic fruit, occasional nuts, and a few leafy greens. Her midwife was a nervous wreck about it, but Linda never had a moment of morning sickness and Tosh was sick only about, oh, three short days during his entire childhood. So who can say what should or shouldn't have been?

As far as we can remember, Tosh didn't eat a bite of meat, dairy, or sugar before going to kindergarten at the two-room schoolhouse in New Mexico, where he quickly caught up to speed with a passion for candy! We were a vegan family for years (meaning that we ate no meat, eggs, or dairy products) and then became committed vegetarians, but then one day when Tosh was about five, the medicine man dropped by our mountain hideaway when the temperature had dropped to well below freezing. He said that we looked as "skinny as skeletons," and he waltzed us through the forest to his shack and promptly stuffed us with his freshly killed deer. "Give-away," he called it. (That's when an animal actually "lays down its life" for a hunter—a fairly common occurrence, or so we were told, among certain Native Americans.) So we tried adding a little wild game to our diets—the original organic meat!— and felt better for it in the cold temperatures. We gradually added very small amounts of organic beef, chicken, and fish to our diet, still living 95 percent of the time on whole grains and lots and lots of organic fruits and veggies.

> Did you know that shoes can be vegan—meaning made without any animal products whatsoever? Actress Natalie Portman designs stylish vegan shoes for a trendsetting company called Té Casan. Plus, she's donating all her profits to the Nature Conservancy!

But the truth is, we love it all—fasting on only water when we're feeling an illness coming on, juicing daily, raw diets, macrobiotic, vegetarianism, and the occasional organic meat dinner. We even enjoy all-out junk-food fests every now and then, preferably with organic chocolate or ice cream. We believe wholeheartedly that life is just better with pizza (preferably with soy cheese), and we don't want to get so caught up in self-imposed rules about what we should and shouldn't eat that we can't enjoy one of life's greatest pleasures—eating! We're not about to give up our favorite meals, and we don't expect you to either. But we do think that eating more consciously makes you and the planet healthier. The good news is that it isn't hard to increase your intake of good food these days, and we think you'll feel the difference in body, mind, and soul when you lessen your meat consumption, which means lessening the stresses that livestock and factory farming puts on the planet.

Make no mistake, we're not talking about forcing you to go from being a Supersize-Me teen to a vegan. We're realistic and it's up to you to find out what diet suits you best. If you decide you want to make changes, go easy on yourself; old habits die hard, especially when it comes to salt and sugar. Just make a start. Try switching over one meal a week or a day and see if eating differently makes you feel better. We think it will.

The big idea is to continually increase the percentage of whole, healthy food going into your body—not to get all worked up because you indulge. Your eating will improve as you get better at choosing restaurants, shopping for good food, or cooking for your friends. And as you become more conscious about the foods you eat, the natural world will shift right along with you.

Remember, though, the opposite is also true—if you're impulsive about your food, only looking for "cheap" and "fast," which we so understand with today's crazy schedules and financial stresses, you'll be eating with the heaviest ecological footprint.

baby steps

The best baby step you can take is to drink more water
and fresh fruit and vegetable juices instead of sodas and
sugary drinks—and to eat more fresh, raw foods, which
means foods that haven't been preserved or cooked in
temperatures above 116 degrees (which destroys valuable
vitamins and enzymes), so that they retain their high
water and nutrient content. Your body is about 70 percent
water. The planet is about 70 percent water. The more
high-water-content foods you can ingest—even up to 70
percent overall—the healthier you're likely to be. Don't take
our word for it—be sure and check in with yourself (no one
knows you better than you!) and your doctor, but that's
been our experience and the experience of many of our
friends, including supermodel and actress Carol Alt, whose
book *Eating in the Raw* we love. If you log on to our site at
www.generationgreenthebook.com, you can check out the
recipes from a few of Tosh's favorite's in her book—things
like raw hummus, fruit parfait, and Kelly's Macadamia
Whipped Cream. They're delicious, and knowing how to
shop for and make a few key raw or organic snacks or
lunches just might help keep you motivated. Then have
your friends over to enjoy them with you!

It's better to buy your fruit and vegetables organic;
today most major supermarket chains carry organic
produce. It's even better if you can make the effort to
shop at local farmers' markets. Eating as a locavore—
consuming locally produced food, usually within about
a hundred miles of where you live—is one of the hottest

trends today. There are lots of benefits to this way of eating—fewer resources needed to transport, process, and package food. Buying local means you'll be treating yourself to some of the freshest food sources around while having the satisfaction of helping the "good guys"—the growers in your area. And when you shop at the local farmers' market regularly, you'll quickly come to find and bond with your new BFF growers. To find out more about local farmers' markets, go to www.apps.ams.usda.gov/farmersmarkets/.

While at the farmers' market, if something isn't clearly labeled as organic, ask. If the seller doesn't seem to want to answer, simple questions such as, "What do you feed your plants?" "How do you keep your plants healthy?" "What do you do about insects?" and "Do you use any chemicals?" will give you a fuller picture.

THE TIP OF THE ICEBERG LETTUCE

All veggies aren't equally good for you. Sure, iceberg lettuce is crunchy, but other than the high water content, which adds value, it's not very nutritious. Did you know that it takes thirty-six calories of energy from fossil fuels to grow and transport one measly calorie of iceberg lettuce? (One head of lettuce has about one hundred calories.) And the United States uses 3.5 million tons of this lettuce every year! Try these easier-to-grow, more nutritious alternatives in your next salad: arugula, endive, kale, parsley, and chard.

eating low on the food chain

If you're like most teens, when you start looking at how to eat more healthfully and consciously, you'll wonder if becoming a vegetarian is a good choice for you.

You may have noticed that some of the most beautiful celebrities are vegetarians! We bet the animals think that people like Carrie Underwood, Pamela Anderson, Daryl Hannah, and Alicia Silverstone are just as beautiful on the inside, too!

You've probably heard that being a vegetarian means that you use less land and fewer resources than a meat eater. If you think that's true, you're mostly right!

It's easy to see why if you boil it down to a simple comparison. You can simply eat legumes, nuts, fruits, grains, and vegetables. Or you can eat the beef, pork, and fowl that were fed the legumes, nuts, fruits, grains, and vegetables. In the first case the only energy used by the planet is the energy to grow, harvest, package, and transport the food. In the second case the planet has to pour a lot of energy not only into growing the animals' food, but also into growing the animals themselves—producing, feeding, killing, processing, packaging, and transporting them so that they end up on your table. In the big picture, that's a lot more impact. You can see how it's therefore much more efficient to eat a plant-based diet directly.

Writer John Robbins tells us in his book *The Food Revolution* that it takes only twenty-three gallons of water to grow a pound of lettuce, and twenty-five gallons for a pound of wheat. But eight hundred fifteen gallons of water are needed for a pound of chicken, and guess how much for a pound of beef? How does 5,214 gallons sound? In fact, if you add up the water used for all of the irrigation to livestock in the United States in one year, you're looking at fourteen trillion gallons!

Of course, the equations aren't always so simple. If, for example, you're a vegetarian who buys highly processed, packaged, concentrated, and refrigerated imports from thousands of miles away, you'll be consuming more resources and energy than someone living in a remote village without an electric refrigerator who eats wild harvested plants and animals. It's not always accurate to assume that a vegetarian has a smaller ecological footprint. But many people become vegetarians for other reasons than just saving energy or trying not to contribute to global warming. Some people stop eating meat because they're big-time animals lovers and can't imagine inflicting harm on one of God's most benevolent creations. That's the case with our buddy Daryl.

green guardian:
AN INTERVIEW WITH DARYL HANNAH

We met movie star Daryl Hannah more than a decade ago in the foothills of Los Angeles at a small sweat lodge ceremony. We knew she was green then: She's wispy thin and unusually radiant in person—everything about her feels somehow unspoiled and natural. But we had no clue we'd have such a comrade in this green goddess whom Tosh first marveled at as the mermaid in love with Tom Hanks's character in *Splash*, and more recently as a badass killer from the *Kill Bill* movies. What most impresses him, though, is that she can afford to live in serious luxury and yet has lived off the grid for many years, with a car that runs on vegetable grease and gets fifty mpg! Tosh also loves her sexy and beautifully shot videos with music that pull you right into her messages about green living. To catch them, log on to www.dhlovelife.com. Also, stay awhile and check out the shopping section of her site— where you'll find everything from a hemp guitar or surfboard to bamboo snowboards to eco-friendly treats for pets.

Daryl made a fundamental decision to change her eating habits after one life-changing encounter. "I became a vegetarian when I was around eleven," she said. "Our family always used to eat at a highway overpass restaurant and I never liked it, so one day I opted to wait in the car. Eventually I got bored and got out to stretch my legs when I saw a truck of calves. I made friends with one in particular, who licked me for twenty minutes. When the driver came out, I asked him what the calf's name was, and he said, 'Veal tomorrow morning at seven o'clock.' That was it. I could never again disassociate what I was eating from the creature it had been. It wasn't a health-related or environmental choice, just a visceral emotional reaction. The fact that being vegetarian also has such a powerful impact on my health and the planetary health is a great bonus!"

Daryl's parents weren't initially supportive of her resolve to become a vegetarian. "My parents sort of ignored my decision, hoping that if they didn't cater to my new dietary needs, I'd grow out of it," she confessed. "I essentially grew up on side dishes, snacks, and junk food. Now I eat much healthier. In fact, it's easy. Except for the rare occasion, there's always something I can eat on every menu.

"I'm almost a vegan. I prefer a raw living food diet when I can do it. I love avocados, and anything from my garden. Everything tastes soooo good when you grow it yourself! My neighbor has a few goats, and sometimes I eat the goat cheese she makes."

Having now spent decades as a vegetarian, Daryl has great advice for teens looking to explore a veggie switch: "Every little bit counts. Once you really think about the ramifications of your choices and actions, you will make wiser decisions. Industrial farming practices are so horrific that if you're not moved by compassion and appalled at the inhumane treatment of the animals, consider the health consequences of the hormones secreted when a creature is terrified and tortured. Those hormones remain in the flesh and you ingest them along with whatever other antibiotics, hormones, medicines, or funky genetic engineering they've done to the creature before it arrives in your supermarket. Also, the meat industry is responsible for a huge amount of the carbon in our atmosphere, increasing global warming. Becoming a vegetarian is the single most effective thing you can do to have a positive impact on the environment."

making sense of your food labels

It can be really confusing shopping for healthier foods at your local grocery store. Here's a guide to help you better understand what these labels are really saying.

Organic: means that a farm and farmer are certified organic. They've earned a diploma for meeting all the requirements in growing, processing, and labeling their food. This isn't an easy process for the growers. It takes a few years for a farm to be certified, and all organic standards have long lists of allowable and banned materials that can or can't be used on the soil or plants, so if something has earned the organic label, it's worth the higher cost!

All-natural: has no legal definition, and whatever it is that you're buying could be legitimately produced by caring people using natural techniques, or the term could be a marketing ploy. Read the fine print to find out if the ingredients in a particular food product really are "natural."

Cage-free: Most factory farmed chickens live in small metal cages under artificial light and are packed so tightly together that they often hurt and even kill one another. For this reason their beaks are usually cut off. The term "cage-free" applies to the chickens and to the eggs they produce and means that the chickens have not been raised in these enclosed pens. Though "cage-free" may be backed up by good intentions, it has no legal definition or enforcement and therefore holds no guarantee that the chickens have been given room to roam.

Free-range: This term applies to beef, pork, and poultry products. The U.S. Department of Agriculture doesn't specify what "free-range" means when it comes to livestock. In order to be certified as free-range, chickens have to have access (however small) to the outdoors (however briefly, even if only for mere minutes). The term "free-range chicken eggs" has no legal definition, however. If you're dealing with a local grower, you can ask how free the range really is, and for how long the animals are able to enjoy it each and every day.

No antibiotics: When animals are packed together in factory farm cages, they frequently fall ill, and when one of them gets sick, the disease often spreads like wildfire. To make up for unhealthy living conditions, antibiotics are added to animal feed or given at regular intervals to prevent disease. Many scientists believe that overuse of antibiotics in livestock and overprescription for humans has led to a surge in antibiotic-resistant illnesses. This means that the antibiotic that used to cure that nasty infection won't work anymore because the infection is caused by a more powerful bug, which means that scientists must now be on the hunt for even more powerful antibiotics to fight it. Many farmers and scientists want to call a halt to this "arms race" by stopping the routine feeding of antibiotics to livestock.

Irradiated: In order to keep your food from going bad, it gets put into a chamber and "nuked," exposed to radioactive isotopes that kill off any bacteria that might cause the food to spoil. However, this process creates free radicals—chemical compounds that wreak havoc in your body. Some researchers claim that irradiated foods show a loss of vitamins and vitality, while they gain carcinogenic and environmental pollutants through radiation exposure. Thankfully, certified organic food is never irradiated.

GMO: stands for genetically modified organism. Farmers have cross-bred plants for centuries, essentially creating new plants with the combined DNA of the parent plants. But GMOs are created differently. In these cases the genetic codes in the plants—often corn, potatoes, canola, soybeans, or rice—are "cut and pasted" using high-tech molecular processes to create new breeds that scientists hope will grow more readily and be more resistant to infection. Farmers, scientists, and consumers have raised a lot of questions concerning the development, patenting, and long-term safety of GMO crops. In southern Mexico for instance, many of the heirloom corn varieties, some grown for many hundreds and possibly thousands of years, have been contaminated by GMO pollen. It's like someone has rewritten the biological history and constitution of the culture, bringing up ethical questions such as: Do we have a right to alter nature's evolutionary time clock on millions of acres of farmland or in remote reserves of agricultural diversity? Do we have a moral obligation to respect genetic boundaries or protect nature's evolutionary rhythms?

Compassionate eating: Okay, this isn't on any store label we know of, but we think maybe it should be! This term comes from our buddy Kreigh Hampbell, who made it up. "I imagine that maybe we could live more like peaceful grazing animals than predators," he says. "To honor all things that make our life possible."

CORN SYRUP AIN'T SO SWEET!

The average American eats forty times more sugar now than a century ago! To keep food prices low and to use up excess corn in the 1970s, the corn syrup industry was born with the help of federal legislation to replace more expensive and less dangerous sugars made from beets and sugar cane. High fructose corn syrup (HFCS) is a combo of fructose and glucose, and a major contributor to obesity, diabetes, and other ailments. Next time you crave candy, try some fresh or dried fruit or nuts instead. That may chill your craving for the sweets and clear your head for homework.

Your Dirty-Dozen List

You won't always be able to make a total commitment to eating 100 percent organic—especially when traveling or when prices are too high. But some foods are safer than others. Here are the infamous Dirty Dozen—the twelve most important foods to buy organic if possible, because the conventional crops are the most heavily sprayed with pesticides: peaches, strawberries, apples, spinach, nectarines, celery, pears, cherries, potatoes, sweet bell peppers, raspberries, and grapes.

If you can't buy organic (and even when you do!), be sure to rinse your produce thoroughly in clean water (some pesticides are water soluble) or use a fruit/veggie wash. Gently rub the skins with your hands, and even use a brush on the tougher surfaces of, say, melons, oranges, apples, and cucumbers to remove imbedded pollutants and microorganisms.

your gas-guzzling dinner

When you're trying to make eco-conscious food choices, you've got to think beyond what you put into your mouth. You'll need to consider how far it had to travel from its birthplace, and how long it took to arrive in your hands.

Experts tell us we're running out of peak oil, and even the president admits that we've got to break our addiction. But that doesn't change the fact that the average piece of food on your dinner plate has traveled a whopping fifteen hundred miles to get there, and often much farther! Yes, you read that correctly. Bizarre, isn't it?

What did it take to get eight ounces of cheese from Holland to your plate? How about those bananas from Costa Rica or Nicaragua? How did those olives on your pizza arrive from Greece? Or that beef from Argentina, lamb from New Zealand, or tomatoes, asparagus, and grapes from Chile? The fact is we eat food shipped from all over the world every day, and the amount of food coming into the United States is climbing—more than seventy billion dollars' worth in 2007.

Other than oxygen, food is our body's main source of energy, but ironically we're squandering energy to produce most of our food. Consider the fossil fuel burned during transportation alone: In that mighty long journey of more than one thousand miles to transport most foods to your plate, know that they're repeatedly loaded and unloaded onto trucks, planes, boats, and trains.

Of course, it takes natural gas and oil to make fertilizers, pesticides, herbicides . . . and more oil still to run the tractors that plant, plow, weed, and harvest. Then even more still to move the trucks that deliver farm supplies and haul the fresh food to the processors, warehouses, supermarkets, convenience stores, airports, stadiums, and fast-food joints. It takes coal, oil, natural gas, hydroelectric power, and uranium to make the electricity to pack, can, refrigerate, freeze, dry, bake, cook, distill, pasteurize, and . . . oh, did we mention package it all?

i'll have that gift wrapped

Bag it, box it, can it, cushion it, shrink-wrap it, bottle it, cap it, wrap it with a tray, double-seal the cap, put six-pack rings around 'em or slide the bottles into a box, shrink-wrap it all again on a pallet for the forklift! Oh, and would you double-bag that big jug of water with the handle already on it, please?

The average American uses more than five hundred plastic bags per year just to carry stuff out of stores. Wow! But haven't you ever gone into a store, bought one tiny item, carried it out in a big bag, and then realized as you were walking out the door that you didn't even need that bag at all? And shopping bags are only the beginning. You're probably stuffing into plastics bags food that's already put into other bags: chips, cookies, carrots, candy, rice, protein bars, meat, bread, tomatoes, lettuce, and beans.

What about going out for coffee or tea and a muffin? Piggybacking on those items are the disposable cup, paper heat shield, cardboard tray, plastic lid, plastic stir stick, sugar packet, cream packet, and that wad of paper napkins.

And what else hitches a ride with your take-out burritos, pad thai, or that seven-layer cake? Plenty of your favorite restaurants still dish it up in Styrofoam trays, cups, and bowls, put a lid on it, then slip it into plastic bags with a fistful of plastic pouches, forks, chopsticks, napkins, coupons, menus, and more plastic bags tied around those foam containers so they won't leak. Are you following the trail of wasted resources here?

The big idea here is that food is a *big* idea. We are feeding at the top of a food pyramid never before imagined. This pyramid is built on gas, oil, coal, fertilizers, pesticides, genetically modified plants, and enormous machinery, with little regard for natural systems. As green citizens, we owe it to the natural world to understand how food is grown, shipped, processed, and packaged and then support the best choices that we have at the time.

Sometimes that choice will mean buying the food grown closest to home, organic if possible. Sometimes that option just might be to include carrying a thermos, travel mug, or dish and fork with you so you don't use throw-away packaging. That's what our friend Julia Butterfly Hill does (see her interview in Chapter Eight), without worrying about what other people think. (Many people tell her they think it's cool, by the way.) Try choosing more products that come in less packaging, or that can return to nature without harm, or be easily recycled into new products.

Styrofoam is an example of engineered waste. It's part of a family of complex technical materials—laminates and composites, plastics, aluminum, paper, steel, and glass—that are born from mining, drilling, and logging, and many of these materials are dependent on toxic chemistry from the cradle to the grave. And Styrofoam doesn't biodegrade; our landfills brim with it. So maybe you'll want to take even bigger steps and ask your local restaurants to consider more eco-friendly containers for takeout. After all, it was consumer demand (and an assist from organizations such as Environmental Defense) that helped the major hamburger chains greatly reduce the volume and environmental impact of their packaging. More on that in Chapter Eight.

green karma

Just as the term "karma" can be said to mean that you get out of life what you put in, we believe that if you conscientiously work to build a healthy regenerative world, you and everyone else will see a better world—a greener world—emerging. Don't slip into the thinking that your actions (indifferences or negativity) don't make a difference. Good things happen because people believe they can make a positive difference. It's all about stewardship, taking care of the things that are entrusted to you. The Dalai Lama said "love, compassion, and tolerance are necessities, not luxuries. Without them humanity cannot survive." Making greener choices about what you stick on the end of your fork has such a huge ripple effect—on the farmers struggling to make organic farming the rule instead of the exception, to the animals who deserve a humane existence, to the workers who harvest and transport everything we consume, to all of us affected by the true costs of bringing our food to our table.

You'll make some sacrifices. You'll spend a bit more to buy organic. You'll skip the instant gratification of the fast-food joint more often. You'll do more home cooking so you don't contribute to the overpackaging problems with takeout. But the green karma of eating well is something you'll feel good about inside and out.

Remember, baby steps, and no one's perfect. Sometimes you're just really going to be jonesing for that pizza or nuggets or fries (or those conventionally grown grapes or strawberries!). But if you do go to fast-food places, please try to cut down and make your footprint as light as possible by not taking the extra ketchup or salsa or napkins. Think about skipping the utensils by ordering finger food such as burritos or tacos (especially tasty veggie ones!). Bring your own mug for the drink. Go to places with recycling bins or take your recycling home with you. Lots of little choices that add up. Easy stuff. The more you do it, the easier it becomes.

Just whatever you do, don't even bother trying to sneak past your mother to have that soda for breakfast!

GREEN BEGINS AT HOME

If you watched the *Live Earth* broadcast on television like we did, you may have seen the mini-film of black helium balloons, each the size of a regular party balloon, being released from a house. Starting inside a kitchen, the camera spied on black balloons bursting forth from every crack and crease, like ghosts in a horror film—slithering out of the coffeepot, blowing up from the power button of the TV, popping out of a tabletop fan, spewing forth en masse from the washer and dryer—anything powered by energy gave them life. And no locked window, door, or chimney could thwart their inevitable escape from the house as they flocked like crows into the sky. Soon the sun was blotted out by the ominous black swarm.

A voice-over announced that each black balloon represented two ounces of greenhouse gases—and that two hundred thousand of them would be released this year from your house, our house, every house in the developed world.

The clip was one of the most powerful images we've ever seen, and it had us spellbound. Quick as it was, it put a very real face on the destructive, normally invisible, nature of our energy use. What made it even more memorable was that these dark ghouls weren't coming from some big, bad, greedy factory somewhere (although that happens too!) but from the sanctity and purity of where we live and love. The *Live Earth* broadcast, more than anything else, hit home for us that our houses are living, breathing entities that must be nurtured, protected, and *rethought*—for both our health and the health of our planet.

"What is the good of having a nice house without a decent planet to put it on?" Henry David Thoreau asked that question more than one hundred fifty years ago, and the question is perhaps even more valid today. We're recognizing that the way in which we build and live in our nice homes has a tremendous cost to our planet.

Stars such as Cate Blanchett, Julia Roberts, Brad Pitt, Adrian Grenier, and Ben Harper are making eco-friendly renovations to their homes—by adding solar panels, installing gray-water recycling, using recycled blue-jean insulation—you name it. Actress Alicia Silverstone's home has energy-efficient appliances (although she loves drying her laundry outdoors), solar panels, and an organic vegetable garden; she filters her water to avoid buying bottles, and reuses old scripts in her fax machine. These celebrities understand that their support calls attention to the cause while greening up their surroundings—a win-win situation. Many families are going green literally from the ground up—building brand-new homes from the latest sustainable materials and energy-conserving or -generating methods—all to help our "decent planet."

That's fabulous, but fortunately you don't need to tear down your home and start from scratch to make a difference. There's so much you can do right now to green your home no matter what kind of house you're living in.

Going green is healthier for the planet; it's also healthier for each one of us. You might be surprised to learn that the pollution inside your cozy walls is often statistically worse than the pollution outside—in some cases by ten times! Smog, a result of chemical reactions primarily made up of the exhaust from cars and industry, is something we all deal with, and even more so when we live in big cities. But because the majority of us spend most of our time *inside* rather than outside, we are constantly inhaling different toxins. You probably don't spend a lot of time thinking about molds, bacteria, viruses, pollen, dust mites, animal dander, and tobacco smoke inside your home, but that doesn't mean you're not breathing them in. And vapors from cooking and heating, as well as from paints, building materials, carpets, and even furniture affect you as well. Ugh. Who knew?

Here you'll find some easy tips for combating those everyday poisons and some general principles of eco-friendly living. For example, maybe you don't yet know (like we didn't, until recently) that a favorite home product—maybe something you even have in your room—is potentially toxic. . . .

the dark side of candles

You know that funny, weird smell when you blow out a candle? Just moments ago your room was filled with a sweet cinnamon-vanilla scent, and now, yeck! What happened? Well, if your candle was made from paraffin, says Patricia Conant, columnist and food writer for www.epicureantable.com, you've been breathing fumes from an inexpensive sludge waste product of the petroleum industry that fills the air with carcinogens such as benzene and toluene—as dangerous as second-hand smoke! Conant adds that these candles (the most common worldwide) can also leave a sootlike residue that contains the same toxins as diesel fuel. You might as well breath the exhaust from a truck. And guess what the wick may be made of? Lead! We don't make lead wicks in the United States anymore, but other countries do, such as China. As the wick burns, it releases toxic particles that you can inhale—especially dangerous to children and pets. So should you give up candles? No way. Just get natural ones made from soy or beeswax. Most people love beeswax candles because they're sweet-smelling and nontoxic—okay, they cost more, but they last three times as long. Plus, you don't inhale poisons. Can you get them at big discount stores? Not yet, although some retailers like Wal-Mart are beginning to stock organic products, so keep up the hope. They may be coming soon.

These are the types of ideas you can use to become a leader in your family and inspire by example. By educating and encouraging one another with creative ideas, you'll make thinking green a more automatic choice.

keeping water from slipping through your fingers

Now that you know more about the growing worldwide water shortage, you may want to think more about how to save water at home. Did you know that the typical household uses more than two hundred sixty gallons of water a day? Whoa! Fortunately, it's not hard to cut that number back by making some simple changes.

In the Kitchen

Which uses less water—washing dishes by hand or doing them in the dishwasher? (You are doing the dishes, right? At least sometimes?) It's hard to say, since it depends on whether you run the water continuously while you're scrubbing at the sink (which is really wasteful, using up to three gallons per minute) or use water more sparingly, as we'll describe below. On average, dishwashers use around seven to ten gallons per use. However, they also use more energy in total, since it takes energy to manufacture the appliance, heat the water, and to wash out the detergent after the cycle's done. Plus, the older the dishwasher is, the more inefficient it is. If your parents are shopping for a new washer, it's best to choose one that has different options, such as "light wash," "air-dry," or "energy saving" cycles, and look for the Energy Star label.

If you do want to use the dishwasher and you don't have one with an air-dry cycle (there will be a button to press), here's a way to get all the benefits while cutting down on the energy you use. After dinner let your dogs pre-clean all dishes first. (Ha! Just kidding. Tosh used to always try to get away with that time-saving maneuver.) Seriously, scrape food and residue into the trash or compost without rinsing (the Department of Energy says you'll save heat and water that way), then run the dishwasher only when it's full (because it uses the same amount of water to wash one dish or twelve). Using phosphate-free detergent requires less water to rinse away and causes less harm to the fish exposed to it at the other end of the sewer system.

After the washing cycle is complete and the drying cycle has kicked in, turn off the machine and open the door a crack or pull out the shelves before you head off to bed. Your dishes will be drying on their own and can be put away first thing in the morning. Remember that while you're watching TV, time flies and it's easy to forget to turn off your machine once the drying cycle starts. So next time you load the dishwasher, look at the clock and write down how many minutes it takes to get from the washing cycle to the drying cycle. Then whenever you load the washer, automatically set your oven timer to remind you to pull out the drawers—this will ensure that you'll make the most of your good green intentions.

Why do energy companies say to run our major appliances at night? Because that lessens energy demands on city resources during peak hours. According to a firefighter friend of ours, however, you *never* want to run your dishwasher or laundry while you're asleep or while you're not home because of the danger of fire and possible flooding. By pulling out the dishwasher drawers *before* bedtime, you won't be leaving the machine unattended while you sleep.

If you're doing the dishes in the sink and you want to be even more water-thrifty, soak them first in a few inches of warm soapy water (again, phosphate-free detergent is more eco-friendly), scrub, then give them a quick rinse in cool water. (It's even easier to do this if you have a two-sink setup.) When you're done with a cooking pot or pan, remember to soak it in water immediately, before the food has a chance to dry. Who wants to spend time, not to mention more water, trying to scrub out last night's dried-on crusty old mac 'n' cheese? *Not.*

Linda's mom was obsessed with saving water, but it wasn't until Linda lived in the forest that she fully understood the effect of hundreds of days in a row without rain—withered plants, dying trees, parched landscapes, panicking animals. The American Indians don't call plain old H_2O "lifeblood" for no reason. When you're forced to do without, you realize that water is as sacred as blood.

When you're learning to become more water-conscious, the kitchen is the best training ground. Here's where you can get really creative with saving water. Follow Linda's example, which we mentioned in the introduction: Let's say your mom asks you to wash the lettuce, spinach, or herbs for the family dinner salad. You've placed the greens in a bowl, filled the bowl with water, soaked the greens for a moment or two, then spun the lettuce. Now, what do you do with this nutrient-filled water? If you act out of habit, you'll pour it down the drain. But if you take just a few extra moments, you can walk it out the front door and throw it into the garden, or perhaps use it to water some thirsty potted plants. Your mom will be so proud!

If you're also washing fruits and vegetables, try rinsing them in a large bowl so that the water doesn't immediately go down the drain. Then, instead of going out to the garden each time you fill the bowl, try pouring each round into a large bucket at your feet and waiting until you're all done before heading outside to feed the yard.

In the Bathroom

Do you run the water while you're brushing your teeth? According to the National Wildlife Federation, you'll save two hundred gallons a month if you keep the faucet off while you're brushing your pearly whites and turn it on only to rinse. Even rocker Slash uses this maneuver! As for brands, try using a health food store all-natural brand of toothpaste that more closely resembles the old practice of using salt and baking soda to clean teeth. These are better than the newfangled concoctions of detergents, foaming agents, synthetic chemicals, and artificial sweeteners that are potentially carcinogenic. Your mouth is the gateway to your body and is made up of very sensitive membranes that absorb pretty much everything you put in there. Just as it's a good idea to watch what passes your lips in terms of food, it's a good idea to rethink what you use to keep your breath truly fresh. Instead of regular mouthwash, which uses a lot of water, alcohol, and additives, try essential oils made of peppermint or cinnamon, or chew on fresh parsley or mint.

You can save water when you wash your face, too. Instead of letting water pour out of the faucet while you're waiting for it to warm up, try washing your face in colder water—that'll wake you up fast! And there's no reason to heat the water up to wash your hands, either. A good soapy lather with cold water rinsing will get your hands plenty clean; studies show that germs don't get killed unless the water's scorching hot, anyway. Keeping the faucet turned to cold saves water and money; houses with electric water heaters spend about 25 percent of energy costs on heating water. (If you haven't done so already, ask your parents to wrap your water heater with insulation. For about six dollars you'll avoid up to 10 percent of your heat loss that way.)

A lot of the water you use in the bathroom goes right down the toilet. Older toilets use more than five gallons per flush! The first generation of low-volume toilets used only 1.6 gallons per use, but a lot of people weren't crazy about them; they didn't always flush everything down on the first try, and that second "courtesy flush" cancels out a lot of the water savings. The good news is that the latest generation of low-volume toilets have fixed all those problems and use only 1.3 gallons per flush. If your folks are looking to replace your toilets, maybe they'll want to put in some of these low-volume ones.

Forgive us for getting personal, but do you flush after every pee? Perhaps you've heard the old saying "If it's yellow, let it mellow; if it's brown, flush it down." That slogan got its start in the 1970s, when California was hit by a nasty drought. It took some getting used to, but the idea caught on. If you're sharing a bathroom with others, or your latest crush could drop by anytime, you might want to take a pass on this hint, but it's something to consider.

Now let's talk about the biggest water waster of all: your daily shower. If you're like the average teen in America, you use at least twenty-five gallons each morning, and that's not even including the days when you're singing the latest T-Pain, thinking about what you'll wear and how you'll dish the latest episode of *Gossip Girl* with your friends at lunch, or falling asleep in there until your mom yells at you to get out! And if you've got one of those fancy showerheads that makes you feel like you're in a rain forest, you're washing even more water down the drain.

Jennifer Aniston should win an Oscar for her short showers—three minutes, to be exact. Ever since learning that people in Africa, on average, use less water in an entire day than she used in one shower, she started setting a timer to alert herself to the self-imposed time limit.

But what if your favorite conditioner takes five minutes to work? How are you supposed to shave or enjoy that great-smelling body wash if you're rushing? Try turning off the showerhead while you work that conditioner in or shave your legs, then do a quick rinse.

And try a little reframing: You don't have to commit to a race against the clock every time you lather up. But small changes add up and every little bit of conservation helps. Showering uses anywhere from two and a half to five gallons a minute. Suppose you shower three hundred times a year. If you showered for one minute less every day, you'd save anywhere from seven hundred fifty to fifteen hundred gallons a year! You might start just by checking in with yourself. If you just want to shampoo your hair, maybe you can do that in the kitchen sink and save a few gallons of water? (Teen girls in the fifties thought a kitchen shampoo more than once a week was a huge luxury.) Girls, have you ever tried pulling your hair back and just washing your bangs? That's an old trick that makes your hair look clean, and it's so much easier than drying your whole head. And the less you shampoo, the more you preserve the natural oils that make hair sleek and shiny. And when you're in a hurry, you can save a lot of time and water with a quick sponge bath. Just grab a natural sea sponge or washcloth and your favorite all-natural body soap or gel, give the trouble spots a fast dab and rinse, and you're good to go!

power to the people

Make Your Appliances Take an Energy Entrance Exam

Looking for a wonderful resource for learning to be more energy efficient? Try your local utility company. Since the average home spends nearly two thousand dollars a year in energy costs, why not encourage your parents to make an appointment for a free energy audit? Your local utility representative can stop by and check to see if your family could save money in the long run by buying newer, more energy-efficient appliances. (For example, the new models of refrigerators—loaded with all sorts of fancy options like in-door beverage access, so you don't have to open up the fridge door just to grab the milk—use up to 75 percent less energy than old models.)

The representative can teach you how cleaning major appliances can make them run more efficiently and he or she can share other tips for shaving money off your electricity bill—not to mention saving a lot of energy. You can also ask your local utility company about the possibility of purchasing your power through wind, solar, and other alternative options.

If you're like Tosh, the appliance you depend on the most is your computer, whether you're IM-ing, checking out the latest YouTube, or, hey, maybe even doing a little homework research. Why not have an eco-friendly computer? Computers that are EPEAT-registered (rated by the Electronic Product Environmental Assessment Tool) have passed Environmental Protection Agency standards for lower levels of cadmium, lead, and mercury. Did you know that laptops use up to 70 percent less energy than desktop computers? Skinny laptops such as the MacBook Air use green materials inside and out, and less than half the packaging. You can even get a solar panel and backup battery to recharge your laptop off the power of the sun. The newest versions of solar-powered laptops can switch over to lithium-ion batteries or electricity so you can still Google on the cloudiest days.

Don't Touch That Dial!

The next time the temperature falls, instead of running over to the thermostat and cranking it up, rethink things. Could you put on a sweater instead? When you go in and out of the house, could you double-check that you shut the door tightly behind you? Instead of keeping the window open to "get some fresh air" while the radiator's churning out heat, could you turn down the thermostat or dash outside for that fresh air break? Sure, you can look to your folks about the big things—insulated windows (a drafty window is like leaving your front door open!), zone heating so you only heat the floor you're on, proper sealing around windows and doors, and so on—but you have your own opportunity to step up too by being more thoughtful about not wasting energy. With petroleum costs soaring, your parents might think the monthly heating bill is scarier than the latest slasher movie, and will appreciate your efforts.

When the weather's hot, do you automatically keep the air conditioner blasting, even when you're out, so things will be nice and chill when you come back? Chillax. Try using just a fan instead. You might want to ask your parents to check your heater or air conditioner filters every month and clean or replace them at least every few months. You may not realize that 10 percent or more of your energy costs can be due to clogged filters keeping the air from circulating freely.

Find a Brighter Idea for Bulbs

They seemed like a bright idea when Edison invented them, but it's a good time to think about replacing the incandescent bulbs in your home. What's the problem with incandescents? They're not very efficient; they use up a lot of electricity and burn out pretty quickly, which means they end up in landfills. In fact, Congress just passed a law at the end of 2007 mandating that incandescents be phased out by 2012. So what should you use instead?

CFL (compact fluorescent light) bulbs use only about a quarter of the energy of incandescent bulbs, but they last ten to fifteen times longer and will save your parents sixty-seven dollars in energy costs over the lifetime of the bulb! Tosh has already made the change in our house. According to the Environmental Protection Agency, if every home in America replaced *just one single incandescent bulb* with a CFL bulb, we'd save enough electricity to light up three million homes! The downsides? Other than the initial extra cost, they're also made with a tiny bit of mercury, which is toxic, so if they break you need to be careful about cleaning up, and when they're used up, you should follow your recycling center's instructions about disposing of them safely or return them to the place where you bought them. The newest generation of CFLs—CCFLs, or cold cathode fluorescent lights—use less mercury, and manufacturers are getting more hip about how to create energy-efficient lights with the warmth of incandescents.

There's another up-and-coming option worth looking into: LED (light-emitting diode) bulbs. Right now they're playing new starring roles in traffic lights, hiking helmets, bicycle lights—even on the Christmas tree in New York City's Rockefeller Center and in the big ball dropped in Times Square on New Year's Eve to usher in 2008! LED bulbs last up to one hundred times longer than incandescents, and unlike CFLs they contain no mercury. However, they're still expensive, they're not as bright as incandescents, and researchers are in the midst of figuring out ways to make the light they cast as appealing as incandescent light.

Tame the Energy Vampires

It's really easy to let electricity zip through our fingers. Ever keep the TV, music player, or lights on while you leave the room because you're going to "be right back"? And then "right back" turns into an hour or an afternoon? How about reframing the situation so that you turn off the power when you leave the room *every* time unless there's a specific reason *not* to? It took some doing, but now Tosh is pretty good about turning off all the lights when he's leaving a room—unless he and his buds are watching one of the *Saw* movies, in which case the energy-saving bulb in his closet's been known to stay on all night.

Ever catch yourself staring into the fridge for long minutes because you can't make up your mind or because you're hoping something magically appeared since the last time you looked five minutes ago? Next time you put your hand on the handle, see if a simple question—What am I really looking for?—can cure that energy-gobbling Open Fridge Syndrome.

Bet you didn't realize your house is filled with vampires. No, not your little brother or the bloodsucking kind. The electricity-sucking kind. Think of all the appliances you've got plugged into the walls—TV, VCR, computer, cell phone charger, iPod charger, hair dryer, coffeemaker, microwave, clock radio, printer, and so on. Of course you know that they suck electricity while you're using them—but did you know that they continue to "sip" electricity even when you're not using them and they're turned off? In fact, according to a spokeswoman for the Environmental Protection Agency's Energy Star program, we spend more than a billion dollars a year powering TVs and VCRs when they're not even turned on! Whether charging or not, the pull from cell phone chargers alone accounts for 1 to 6 percent of our nation's electricity use.

Manufacturers are developing new models of electronics that aren't such energy vampires, but in the meantime, you have some choices. Of course you don't want to have to unplug your clock radio, microwave, or VCR every moment you're not using them—who wants to have to reprogram all those timers? But you can unplug your cell phone charger, iPod charger, and small appliances like coffeemakers and toasters when you're not using them. (Keep at it; it took a while for Tosh to teach himself this new habit. He'd forget that he'd have to plug the charger back in and would wake up the next morning to find his cell phone deader than last year's UGGs.) And if you're not going to be using your printer for a while, it makes sense to unplug that, too.

If your family's planning to go away for a few days, it's a good idea to go around the house to see what you can safely unplug. Our friend Ed Begley, Jr., installed one switch by his front door that he flips off every time he leaves the house that takes care of all those outlets at once! Often called a "House Off" switch—and more common in Europe—this affordable invention allows you to turn off all nonessential electronic items in your home from one switch. Of course your refrigerator, fish tank heater, or any other appliances that need to run continuously aren't hooked into the system. (And if your family uses a timer to turn lights on and off automatically while you're away so passersby think someone's home, you wouldn't hook those into the "House Off" switch either. Just power those lamps with CFLs!) Sounds tricky, but it's a snap. Just push the button when you leave home and turn off all those sipping electronics. When you get home, one flip of the switch makes it seem as if you never left.

Buy Better Batteries

Flashlights, portable music players, digital cameras, PDAs, bicycle lights—they all run on batteries. And where do the fifteen *billion* batteries we use each year end up? You guessed it: landfills, where the mercury and mercury compounds inside them leak out and poison people and wildlife. A greener choice? After you've used up the regular batteries you've got, hold on to them for recycling (your sanitation department can tell you how, or contact the Rechargeable Battery Recycling Corporation at www.rbrc.org for a location near you where you can drop off used batteries), and then buy rechargeable ones. They cost more up front, but you can recharge and reuse them over and over, sometimes hundreds of times. If you've got to use regular batteries, try to buy the mercury- or cadmium-free batteries, which are much less toxic to the earth. Lithium batteries too often require fewer batteries for the same job because they last a lot longer.

set yourself up for recycling success

It's easier to recycle your paper, plastic, and glass when you've got the right containers all set up for it. Look around your home. Is there a handy place in the kitchen, pantry, or garage where you can put bins? By placing a bin up in your room, you can stow old homework and study sheets right away so they won't end up in the regular trash. Can a special recycling container fit next to the trash can under your desk or in your closet? Tosh puts all his recyclables into one container in his room, then walks it down to the garage and separates them into the different bins on his own before collection days.

We wish we could tell you that there's one and only one definitive list of what you can and can't recycle, but unfortunately, the only way to know for sure is to call your local recycling center or check online; it all depends on where you live and the kind of recycling facilities in your area. You don't want to carefully fold all your cereal and pizza boxes flat and pop them into the recycle bin, only to discover that your local center can't use them—*and* that they have to spend time and money pulling them out of the recyclables. Once you find out, you might want to send e-mails to friends and family in your area, and let your school know too. In some areas the local recycling center mails out helpful flyers outlining the dos and don'ts for where you live, or a handy magnet to stick on your fridge. You may be able to arrange for special pickups of, say, corrugated boxes that don't belong in the regular recycling bins (ask to make sure they won't end up with the regular trash), or you can drop off things like phone books at the recycling center for special disposal.

Recycling paper is even easier if you don't let it into your house in the first place. Picture an endless forest of one hundred million trees. Now picture it shredded and coming through your mail slot, and the mail slots of everyone you know. That's how many trees are used to create the junk mail we generally lug right from the mailbox to the paper recycling bin. Sale circulars, credit card come-ons (yep, they want teenagers, too!), catalogs for stuff you can't live without, even though you never even knew it existed before. According to www.catalogchoice.org, nineteen billion catalogs alone are mailed to American shoppers each year. Wouldn't it be great to save all those trees by stopping those unwanted deliveries? And of course it's not just trees you'd be saving if you could junk the junk. According to Sue Shaw of www.sort.org, if you could stem the tide at your address for just one year, you'd also save one hundred forty gallons of water (used to make the paper pulp from trees), keep ninety-two pounds of carbon dioxide from being dumped into the air, and save your mail carrier from hefting forty-one pounds of paper!

The mission at www.donotmail.org, www.proquo.com, and www.catalogchoice.org is to help you take your name off unwanted mailing lists and drop-kick all those unsolicited offers. But you like browsing through your catalogs? Just enjoy the view from the Web. As you'll see in Chapter Four, ordering online is greener. And for the magazines you love, did you know that buying them through subscription is actually better for the environment than buying them at the newsstand? How could this be? Because more than half of all magazines for sale at newsstands don't actually find a home and end up getting hauled to the trash.

In the kitchen, please make sure to rinse and shake dry your bottles, cans, and plastics before you toss them into the recycle bin; bits of food sticking to recyclables can make them moldy and unable to be recycled.

Stock up on reusable heavy-duty plastic, canvas, or hemp tote bags so you can cut back on the flimsy plastic ones from stores. (See if your grocery store recycles used plastic bags.) You may want to stash some in each car, tuck one under the seat of your bike, and have one in the closet ready to grab if you're heading out on foot. The hardest part of using reusable bags is remembering to take them with you—we can't count the number of times we've left them in the car and had to double back to get them!—but with practice it becomes a habit.

Beyond Paper, Glass, and Plastic: the Big Picture

Recycling's about giving a new life to old things. Why limit it to the paper, glass, and plastic you put out on the curb? Take a fresh look around your house with green eyes. What else can you recycle that other people might appreciate? As you give what you no longer want to others, they in turn can slow down their consumption—a great way to reduce and reuse. We used to be a big garage-sale-ing family—a great opportunity to get rid of our old stuff and make a few nickels and dimes (actually, sometimes hundreds of dollars). But that got old and we decided we wanted to give more, not get more. Now every two months we clean out our closets, drawers, and cabinets and donate whatever we can. Donation: What a great way to recycle! We never worry that we've given away too much, because the good karma seems to send us what we need. Check this out for cool: Recently Linda gave Tosh the garage so he could turn it into his senior-year "bachelor pad." Tosh wanted his buds to be able to hang out there and play Ping-Pong and listen to music, so he got an inexpensive but nice couch from Goodwill—recycling!—but really wanted a second couch too. The very next day we spotted a fantastic couch being tossed out by a neighbor across the street—and it was exactly the small size Tosh needed. Recycling karma to the rescue!

It's an easy call giving away the things you've outgrown, but what about the stuff that still fits that you haven't worn in a while? Should you hold on to it? Or what about the toys, games, or books you don't use anymore but still like? There's a saying from a theologian named Justo González that might help you make up your mind: "When you hold on to something that you don't need or use, you're keeping it from its rightful owner."

Sure, there are a few things you'll want to hold on to for sentimental reasons—a few choice stuffed animals, some treasured books. But it feels good finding the next "rightful owner" for the things you don't really treasure anymore. For example, some children's hospitals are happy to have gently used stuffed animals so a young patient will have one to cuddle far away from home. (Call and ask, since some hospitals want only new stuffed animals.) Could a local homeless shelter use the games, toys, clothes, or sports equipment you don't want? Could you get together with friends and swap clothes so you can freshen up your wardrobe without spending a dime? At the end of the Valencia High School tennis season, Tosh likes to go through his tennis clothes and donate them to the team so the coach can pass them along.

Or you can "freecycle": take possessions you're ready to pass along to a place where they're most likely to find their new owner—which we'll talk more about in Chapter Four. When you visit a freecycle event, everything you see there is free for the taking, but trust us—the real fun comes in knowing you're finding a good home for what you no longer need.

be green when you clean

If you check under the kitchen sink, chances are good that you'll find a lot of cleaning products filled with chlorine, bleach, and other additives that are harmful to the environment. It's pretty easy to find out which ones are dangerous—the words "poison," "danger," "keep out of reach of children," and "warning" are usually in boldface lettering right on the bottles! Not only do all those toxins end up in our environment, but the bottles—most of which can't be recycled—clog our landfills. Phosphates in detergents bubble up not only in our sinks, dishwashers, and washing machines, but in our streams, too.

Fortunately, more and more nontoxic natural cleaning alternatives are hitting the market. Look for labels including "no petroleum products," "phosphate-free," and "biodegradable." Green Seal is a nonprofit environmental organization that has been certifying products as meeting its strict environmental standards since 1992, so if you spot a product with the Green Seal, it's generally eco-friendly. Better yet, you can use the very same products that our great-grandparents used to keep their homes fresh and clean:

- baking soda (check the side of the box for fascinating uses you'd never think of)
- vinegar
- lemon juice
- borax

You don't need to use harsh cleansers to clean the sink, countertops, or bathtub—usually a paste of baking soda and a good coarse scrubbing sponge will get out stains and deodorize just as well. Squeeze the juice from a lemon and mix it with baking soda to shine up copper pots. If it's your job to dust the furniture, try mixing two parts olive oil and one part lemon juice (without pulp) and rubbing with an old rag. Baking soda and a damp sponge will clean most pen and marker spots off wallpaper. Next time you wash the windows or your windshield, use vinegar diluted with water and old newspapers instead of paper towels. (No, the newsprint doesn't run.) Or pour vinegar instead of bleach into the toilet to remove stains. No more horrible fumes while you do your part to keep your house clean! We could write a whole book about how to make your own household cleaners out of safe, all-natural ingredients—but we don't need to, since there are so many excellent books and websites already available. (What a cool present to give your mom or dad—a guide to all-natural cleaning tips and a book of homemade coupons they can redeem to get you to do the cleaning!)

In our household we use Begley's Best—the eco-friendly brand of cleaners sold by actor Ed Begley, Jr., which are made from all-natural biodegradable ingredients like extracts of pine, palm extract, citrus, maize, fermented sugar cane roots, and olive seeds. Ed is surely Hollywood's most famous and committed environmentalist. Two decades ago he was riding buses to auditions in Los Angeles—not an easy thing in a town so dedicated to car culture. When Linda and Ed met up last year at a vegan restaurant in Studio City on another eco-friendly project, Ed didn't disappoint and showed up on his bicycle. People on the sidewalk stared, but Ed didn't notice. When you're used to rolling up to the red carpet on your two-wheeler, a few starstruck shopkeepers aren't a big deal.

Ed pedals to his own rhythm, and people find it riveting. His green show, *Living with Ed,* an HGTV hit in its second season, shows the decidedly unglamorous side of living a low-consumption life in Hollywood—something his wife humorously fights at nearly every turn. (Can you blame her?) One of our idols, Bobby Kennedy, Jr., a longtime friend of Ed's, has said, "Ed has a greater sense of social obligation than anyone else I know. He's like a West Coast cadet who gets up every morning and says 'reporting for duty.'" Ed's enthusiasm and commitment are infectious; no wonder people are copying his green antics!

We sat down to ask Ed a few questions about his passion for pasting his face on green home-cleaning products.

squeaky green:

AN INTERVIEW WITH ED BEGLEY, JR.

"I wanted to do—in my small way—a version of what Paul Newman's done with Newman's Own products: to have a line of good products, and to give lots of money away to good causes." Never mind that Paul's given away two hundred million dollars to charities, we gently reminded him. "Oh, I'm chasing you, Paul!" Ed laughs. "He says he hasn't the slightest idea how he's been so successful. I say that it doesn't hurt that his stuff tastes so good! You can't exactly eat mine, but I'm doing what I can."

It's not like Ed's products aren't popular; they're selling in one hundred stores, and he still has time to hand-deliver his wares. "I don't have employees. It's just me, which is why I can give so much to charity. One time Kathy Najimy ordered a box of stuff and I rang her doorbell with the box in my hand, and she was like, 'What are you doing delivering your own stuff?' The personal touch makes all the difference." At first his products sat on the shelf at Whole Foods and didn't move. "People didn't know if it was a joke, seeing my face on the bottles. I set up a booth on weekends. People bought the first bottle from me, the second because it's a good product."

For teens looking to swap out the most hazardous cleaning products in their homes, Ed recommends: "Get rid of the tile cleaners and the ammonia window cleaners. We have substitutes, with ingredients like water, coconut, and alcohol. Ammonia's fumes are noxious—irritating to the eyes, nose, throat, and lungs." According to *National Geographic*'s Green Guide, which recommends Begley's Best products, ammonia poses an added threat in that it can react with chlorine to produce lung-damaging gases, and is responsible for recent incidents of fish die-offs in Oregon.

"Think about it—who spends the most time in the tub? Babies and children. Their bodies are susceptible to harmful chemicals, whose toxins are easily absorbed through the skin and make their way through the bloodstream."

Cleaning a home just might feel like a snap when you compare it to the space he used to clean—the air over Los Angeles! Ed became an environmentalist by working to clean up smog in the 1980s. "I bought my first electric car in 1970. I was fed up with the smog and wanted to do something. Even though we have a lot of work to do on air quality, we have come a long way. We have four times the cars since 1970, but only half the smog!"

Ed loves being a quiet green rebel and says that some of his favorite fans from his green show are Republicans who disagree with him politically (and tell him his beautiful wife could do better than him) but then ask him funny questions— like how they can catch rainwater from their roofs! "I'm proud to say that about 40 percent of the e-mails I receive are from self-proclaimed red state Republicans. Everyone wants to do their part these days to clean up the air and lessen our dependence on foreign oil."

His best sage advice for any teen trying to go greener? "Start small and build. You don't run up Mount Everest. You get to base camp, you get acclimated, and then only climb as high as you can."

When you make the shift to greener cleaning products, remember not to just pour the old toxic stuff down the drain or toss it into the trash. Call your local recycling center to find out how you can bring in these products for safe disposal.

let your plants do the scrubbing . . . *no kidding*!

While you're helping clean the rest of the house, why not
let your houseplants clean the air? In 1989, NASA teamed
up with the Associated Landscape Contractors of America
to study whether common household plants could help
purify the air. Turns out, they do a pretty great job! They
basically act as living, breathing air filters—absorbing
carbon dioxide and releasing oxygen. Some did better
at scrubbing benzene from the air. Others excelled at
removing formaldehyde or trichloroethylenes. NASA
compiled a list of the top fifteen air-purifying plants, all
of which are widely available at your local nursery, your
home improvement center, or maybe even your grocery
store. Tosh's favorite is the spider plant because it seems
that no matter how long it takes him to remember to
water the poor thing, it's still miraculously green and *alive.*
But you might want to fill your rooms with other popular
living filters like English ivy, philodendron, dracaena, peace
lily, or snake plant. The study suggests that you scatter
at least fifteen of these plants around a home of about
eighteen hundred square feet. It's best to use a variety of
plants in pots at least six inches in diameter.

greener room renovation

So you finally got permission from your parents to redo
your room; those cartoon characters on your walls and
bedspread just aren't cutting it anymore. Here are some

ideas for how to renovate any room so that it's cooler and greener, too.

Changing the Walls Around Us

According to the Environmental Protection Agency, on average the air inside your own home is three times more polluted than the air outside. One of the reasons is VOCs—volatile organic compounds—such as heavy metals or formaldehyde. VOCs are found in a lot of paints and cleaning solvents. Think of the smell of a freshly painted room. Pretty strong, right? Those fumes actually tell you that toxic VOCs are off-gassing—being released into the air. And the process doesn't stop once the paint is dry; VOCs continue to be released very slowly even years after you've painted—and when you open up the window to air out the smell, those VOCs contribute even more freely to ozone depletion.

VOCs, volatile organic compounds, contribute to "sick building syndrome," which affects people in many office buildings and residences and can be generated not just by paint but also by carpets, laminated furniture, and photocopiers.

So what can you do? Shop for nontoxic or low-toxic paints. As more paint manufacturers have come to appreciate the health benefits of greener paints, the costs have been coming down, and it's easy to find greener paints in all the major stores. They come in three categories: natural (which include paints made from milk and clay), low-VOC, or no-VOC. Look for paints that meet the Green Seal standard or are certified by LEED (Leadership in Energy and Environmental Design, an organization that sets standards for environmentally sustainable construction). Buy the minimum amount that will get the job done, so you don't have to store leftovers. And if you need more than a day to finish the job, wrap up your brushes and paint pan with plastic bags so air won't dry up the paint and you won't need as much water to clean everything afterward.

If you're not using "green" paint, be especially careful not to just toss your leftovers into the trash. Check with your local recycling center; they'll tell you which days you can bring in toxic paint for safe disposal.

If you need to remove wallpaper before painting, you want to avoid the formulations with those scary warning labels. Look for nontoxic, biodegradable wallpaper removers, or try mixing equal parts hot water and white vinegar and saturating the paper with a sponge. You could also rent a steamer, which works like a steam iron to soften up old paste so you can peel the wallpaper away.

Dressing Up Your Windows

Shop for curtains made of fabrics from organic cotton or highly renewable materials, such as hemp, bamboo, Tencel, Modal, or recycled material—or if you're crafty, sew your own! Organic fabrics have been made without harmful pesticides, dyes, or bleaches. Fabrics made from

sustainable crops put less stress on the environment.
To save energy, shop for curtains and blinds specially
designed to keep heat in. It might seem obvious, but open
up your blinds when the sun's shining to bring more of
that natural warmth inside. And remember to close them
when it gets dark so that warm air will have less chance of
disappearing into the night.

Bringing the Forest Inside

Looking for a new computer table or chair? Shop for
furniture labeled FSC-certified, which means that the
Forest Stewardship Council—an organization of loggers,
foresters, environmentalists, and sociologists dedicated
to sustainable forestry—has given it the thumbs-up.
Companies who receive FSC certification have taken
steps to limit the logging of old-growth forests, to protect
valuable forestland, and to adhere to fair labor practices.
The FSC supports the Rainforest Alliance's Rediscovered
Wood and SmartWood programs, which use salvaged or
recycled wood instead of cutting down more trees. It also
supports the Scientific Certification Systems (SCS), which
certifies that the wood contains no formaldehyde, no
VOCs, or uses recycled or reclaimed wood.

   If you can't get certified wood, avoid woods from
old-growth forests, such as redwood and Douglas fir,
or tropical hardwoods like mahogany and teak, which
are being overlogged and take many years to regrow.
There are a lot of fantastic furniture designs made from
recycled plastic wood substitutes like Plastic Lumber and
Polywood.

Or how about hopping down to the used furniture or antiques store and getting a one-of-a-kind piece of furniture to make your room truly unique?

Not-So-Magic Carpets

Ever walked into a home where they've put down new carpet? That smell is—you guessed it—VOCs again! So if you want a new carpet or rug to perk up your room, look for natural wool, organic cotton, jute, or hemp, or shop the thrift stores or swap with a friend for a used rug. Better yet—look for the latest technology in sustainable "cradle to cradle" carpet by the Shaw brand, which doesn't off-gas and is made so that the waste produced during the manufacturing process—while growing organic cotton, for example—can actually be used to nourish the environment by leaving nutrients behind in the soil. And every fiber of the finished product can be reused or recycled.

Better Fabrics and Bedding

It's exciting how many manufacturers are offering fabrics, slipcovers, sheets, and bedding made from organic cotton and bamboo grown without harmful pesticides or fertilizers. They're so soft, and come in cool colors, too. Please consider taking your old sheets to the nearest shelter if they're in decent shape. If not, you can cut them up for rags to use for dusting.

Organic pillows and mattresses in the bedroom can also cut down on allergies and other maladies because they rarely contain traces of the pesticides, fertilizers, flame retardants, or residue from toxic manufacturing processes that can irritate sensitive nasal passages and lungs. They're more expensive but worth investigating. After all, you're spending about eight hours a night with your body in direct contact with these surfaces!

greening your laundry

You know how you have that one pair of really great jeans that just fit and feel the *best*? Ever need to wear them immediately and because they're in the hamper, you toss them into the washer or dryer all by themselves? We've all done it, but it's not the greenest choice. A better idea? Plan ahead so you always run a full load of laundry—using cold water takes the least amount of energy—and use a phosphate-free detergent. You can hand-wash those jeans or, at the very least, run them on cold at the "hand wash" setting in the machine. Always set the machine for the most efficient temperature and moisture-sensing settings and run the load after peak hours when you can.

Dryers use up a lot of energy. If you're going to use one, remember that simple things like clearing or even washing your lint trap can save loads of energy because the air can flow more freely and the clothes will dry more quickly. There's nothing like the smell of laundry that's been dried in the fresh air, so if you have a yard, you might try line-drying your clothes. Even if you just have a small clothesline in the basement or pantry, you'd be amazed at how many clothes you can dry. (You can almost see your workout-wear dry, it's so quick!) If you do use the dryer, did you know that you can buy great-smelling natural dryer sheets at health food stores? They're amazing! If you want to use up your "regular" ones first, try using a quarter or half of a sheet with every use, or reuse the same dryer sheet several times; it'll still do its job.

A lot of clothing labeled "dry-clean only" can in fact be gently hand-washed. (We recommend all-natural liquid soaps.) If you must dry-clean something, find a wet dry cleaner, which uses only cold water, or a green dry cleaner. Regular dry cleaners use solvents with a lot of VOCs. That's what that "clean" smell is—perc, or perchloroethylene, made of chlorine and identified as a "probable" human carcinogen by California's Proposition 65. Basically, it stinks, and if you're stuck picking up this kind of cleaning, air it out in the backyard or in the garage before bringing it inside.

Tosh is really into stepping out in clean, fresh white Ts and would prefer to change several times a day, but he's trained himself to change only if his clothes really need it. Also, he's more careful with the clothes he's wearing (so he won't need to use bleach or spot remover). Most important, at the end of the day he hangs up the clothes that aren't dirty so he can get another wearing out of them instead of simply tossing them into the hamper because he doesn't feel like fishing around for a hanger.

greener inside for a greener outside

What's the most-used countertop appliance in your kitchen? In ours it's become the tabletop composter! This is a small bucket with a tight-fitting lid and a handle. We keep it lined with newspaper or a used paper towel, and we dump coffee grounds, tea leaves, vegetable trimmings, plate scrapings, egg shells—anything that isn't fat, meat, or bone. You can even add the lint from your dryer's lint trap! When the bucket fills up, we take it outside and dump it into the larger composter we've got in our backyard. We stir it every now and then, mix in some dirt from our garden, and in a few months we've got the most amazing compost—rich, clean-smelling humus we can use for planting our vegetable garden, repotting houseplants, or sprinkling around our bushes and shrubs to give them a fresh shot of nutrients. This is a fantastic way to see the benefits of recycling in your own home.

Some folks make a wigglier kind of compost—from worms! When you're "vermicomposting," you make or buy a special bin, fill it with shredded newspaper, dump in a pound of worms (that's about eight hunded to one thousand worms), and feed the compost bin with your table scraps, etc. In three or four months those busy worms will produce castings—a nutrient-rich substance you can use just like regular compost to repot your plants, give your garden a boost, or sprinkle around the yard.

greener pet care

If you're like Tosh, you care very deeply about your pets! Here are some great tips so you can feed and care for yours in ways that benefit them as well as the environment.

Pet Food

As long as you're exploring better ways to feed yourself (as we discussed in the last chapter), why not give your pets the same cuisine makeover?

Tosh's dogs eat organic lettuce, carrots, celery, or spinach every day along with organic, all-natural dog kibble and olive oil. (Double-check with an expert about what you can feed your particular breed.) We feed our dogs Newman's Own Organics dog food—made, like organic people food, without harmful pesticides, fertilizers, or other additives—and are pleased to see that many other companies are also starting to develop organic options for pets. In fact, the market for organic pet food is growing three times faster than the market for organic people food! Yes, it costs more than regular nonorganic food, but if enough people buy organic food for their cats and dogs, prices will fall just as they are for organic people food. And you can always make the case to your folks that a little more money invested in a healthy diet (prevention) just might save a whole lot of money down the line in veterinary bills.

Pet Care

We bathe Tosh's dogs in toxin-free shampoo and comb them often with flea combs, which remove fleas without chemicals. We don't use the flea collars, shampoos, or bombs that are filled with insecticide. The "acute hazard warning" labels that warn you to "avoid contact with skin" and "don't inhale!" make for some disturbing reading. A friend of ours has had a lot of success keeping down the population of ticks and fleas with all-natural collars, but often a healthier, more vitamin-rich diet can do wonders. Garlic, too, often helps keep fleas at bay because dogs release the smell through their skin and fleas just don't have the appetite for it. However, this is really a subject to talk with your vet about, since not all natural collars work the same way, and what's most effective for dogs might not be so great for your cats. We prefer talking with holistic vets to learn about the many options.

The Pentagon has had to issue several warnings to its service members not to use flea or tick collars shipped to Iraq and Afghanistan by concerned family members trying to protect their loved ones from insects. "Prolonged exposure to the collars may produce toxic effects in humans."

Dog Duty

If you're blessed enough to be the proud companion of a lovable dog or two (or, in our case, three), you're most likely accustomed to stuffing your pockets with plastic bags before heading out to take your dog for their all-time favorite thing . . . a walk! If you do this once or twice a day, you've used thousands of plastic bags to pick up their waste over the years. Instead, try carting around the more environmentally responsible metal or plastic pooper-scooper. If you find plastic bags easier to carry—especially when you've got more than one leash in your hands—why not reuse your old broccoli or lettuce bags from the grocer?

Here's another idea: To supplement those bags from the market, think about trying to use the same plastic bag twice on the same walk. (Not recommended for the waste of large dogs, however, unless you're especially coordinated in the art of handling flimsy plastic bags in all types of weather.) You can also try bringing along scraps of old newspaper or drying your old, soggy paper towels and bringing them along with you to pick up a second pile for that same bag. Personally, we do all of the above, and purchase biodegradable doggy bags to carry as well— doing our doggone best to live green!

Some grocery and health food stores already carry biodegradable plastic bags, and if yours doesn't, make a request with the store manager. You can also purchase biodegradable poop bags from www.ecoanimal.com or www.greenfeet.com.

GUILT-FREE
SHOPPING

We've all heard the saying "Some of the best things in life are free," and of course we know that we should be shopping less at the mall, right? If not to save money, then certainly to lessen our impact on the planet by consuming fewer resources. But while we can and *should* cease our material binges, no one expects you to go on a total shopping fast. In this chapter we'll look at the overall picture of consumerism, and then offer you tips for how your purchase dollars can help you live more in alignment with your new Earth-friendly resolve.

back to basics

For fun let's put our green contact lenses on again and go back to nature for a little refocusing. You can do this in your mind, but having a real-life visual makes a bigger impact, so if you can, step out into your yard or, better yet, get yourself in nature for a walk or hike. Ideally, focus where you can see primarily just earth, sky, trees, rocks—and water and animals, if you can. Now look at the trees, the dirt, the rocks, the water, and the rhinos (just kidding), and imagine that the whole planet looks just like this, as it did once a very, very long time ago. Just nature, all around. Nothing more. Nothing less.

Next think about your car, your house, your room, your TV, your Nikes, your CDs—imagine everything you own piled high in front of you in the dirt or grass. Think about it: Where did all this stuff originate? Where did the metal and plastic and glass in your car come from? The wallboard and carpet and furniture of your room? The wires and buttons and screen of your TV? The leather and cloth and plastic of your Nikes and CDs? Yep, it all came from this—the idyllic scene around you . . . from the sky and dirt and trees and rocks and water and animals. Everything you own—heck, everything you can *see* in the man-made world—used to be just gaseous, dirty, fibrous, rocky, wet, wild, or hairy raw materials.

One of the greatest challenges we face is that our consumption is wildly out of pace with the amount of natural resources we've got left. If we keep consuming at today's rate, it'll take *two* earths to supply the natural resources we need, according to the 2006 Living Planet Report by the World Wildlife Fund and the Global Footprint Network. And, they add, if other nations lived like we do in America, it would take *five* planets to support us. Right now, with the rapid expansion and Westernization of many third world countries, especially China and India, you can see why some scientists worry that we're living on borrowed time.

So it makes sense that if we poison or deplete all of the ingredients that make up our natural world—the components of modern life—we won't be able to sustain our present level of comfort. It's like making a sundae. If you've got only a half of a scoop of vanilla ice cream left— the chocolate and strawberry flavors are gone, the banana's rotten, and the cherry and nuts are stale—what are you left with? A wimpy cup of one measly flavor. No more sundaes.

So let's get a handle on our consumption and restore balance to the natural world so that our home—our mama—can continue to parent us. What can you do as a member of Generation Green to help lessen Mama's burdens? Start with learning how to shop more responsibly. We hope you've already started lessening your carbon footprint by following up on some of the suggestions in earlier chapters. This chapter will help you build on that momentum.

before you head to the mall

We've grown up in a powerfully consumer-driven culture, but it was only a few generations ago that world wars and the Depression left widespread shortages and financial hardship. People scrimped and saved for everything. The current generation of teens, on the other hand, has experienced greater ease and financial freedom than perhaps any other teen generation in world history. That translates into the ability to buy what you want when you want it, which has given you an expanded sense of freedom and creativity that's really, really easy to get used to.

Have you ever had an impulse to buy something—maybe while watching TV—only to grab your keys on impulse to race off and buy it? Do you ever think about *why* you want what you want? Could it be that you're being influenced by outside sources you're not even totally aware of? According to Citizens for Independent Public Broadcasting, the average kid watches more than a thousand hours of TV every year (on par with the amount of time they spend in school!) and sees more than twenty thousand commercials. And if you think about it, every one of those commercials is trying to influence your thoughts and get you to buy, buy, buy. No wonder spending money on things we don't necessarily need or even keep for that long is such a tough habit to break.

So when it comes to shopping, it might be good to pump the brakes a little bit and go back to the five Rs of Chapter One and reduce, reuse, recycle, rethink, refuse.

When Tosh—the ultimate I-want-it-now kid—has the urge to buy something, he's learning to stop, take a breath, and run through this checklist.

REDUCE

- Can I use less of what I already have instead?

REUSE

- Is there any way to borrow or rent what I want?
- Can I buy a used or refurbished version of this product?

RECYCLE

- Do I know someone who can trade me something I want for something I have that they want?

RETHINK

- Is this a want or a need? How do I know?

- What's influencing my planned purchase? TV? Friends?

- Am I really going to wear or use this next year?

- Can I list five good reasons I have to have this product?

- Have I researched the most eco-friendly producer or carrier of this product?

- Can I purchase the product I need without packaging?

- How much more am I willing to pay to buy a "green" version of what I want?

- Is it really cost-efficient to buy more of this product, or does it just encourage me to overbuy?

- If I have to get it now, could I bike or walk to the store?

REFUSE

- Can I go one week/month/year without this product?

- If I can go that long, how about I just skip it altogether?

If the list sounds a little long, that's the point! The goal here is to stop that autopilot that says, I want it. I've got the money. *Let's hop in the car and go get it!*

how green is that company?

If you do decide to get something after all, how can you buy it green? Have you noticed how many companies are talking about their greenness on TV commercials or ads in magazines and newspapers? With everyone jumping on the green bandwagon, it can be hard to tell which companies are coming from an honest, truly green place and which ones are using the green platform as more of a PR tool. For instance, a company might have a great line of organic products you like, but if they're using a lot of petroleum or dangerous chemicals (or testing on animals) for other product lines, does that work for you? You might want to consider using your dollars in support of a different, greener company that's perhaps more consistent throughout all of their product lines and not just "greenwashing" their image with a few key items. Corpwatch.org gives out Greenwash awards every two months to the companies that put more effort into looking eco-friendly than actually creating products that lessen their impact on the environment. Nominations come from readers. The market is being forced to become more transparent, thankfully, but until things are really clear, it's wise to wear your green contact lenses as you walk through the world as a consumer.

Doing your homework by logging on to a company's website and doing some investigative researching online will hone your instincts and make it a little easier to find out which companies are truly green.

Here are a few of the resources we use to help us make sense of it all.

You can start by searching online through Co-op America's National Green Pages, which sells itself as the nation's only directory of screened and approved green businesses. Check their website www.coopamerica.org /pubs/greenpages to search for green businesses by category and state. You can also find cool tips and essays on living greener.

The gift guide at www.treehugger.com rates the greenness of the products it recommends according to light green, medium green, and dark green, with lots of creative suggestions organized by categories like "for the geek/fashionista/animallover/outdoors lover."

We also can't speak highly enough of the product reviews at *National Geographic*'s Green Guide, which you can find at www.thegreenguide.com.

You've heard the saying that you can't always judge a book by its cover, and that's a two-way street. It could be shortsighted to assume that a company using large amounts of natural resources doesn't have good intentions or do right by the environment in other ways. For example, Peter Vegso, the publisher of Linda's first book, is also the publisher of the international bestselling *Chicken Soup for the Soul* series, including the popular *Teenage Soul* line. As the series started breaking records on the bestseller lists years ago, Jack Canfield, the author of the books (in partnership with Mark Victor Hansen), told Linda that their consumption of trees was keeping him up at night, despite the books' obvious healing effect on readers. Thus, planting trees—millions of them—became a way for the publisher and authors to join forces to feel proactive about helping offset some of their paper consumption.

jump into the car
or log on to the web?

Meeting everyone at the mall can be a lot of fun, but there's no question that hopping into the car to get there stamps more of your carbon tread onto the planet. That's why Tosh and Linda love shopping online. No matter if a bad hair day's got you hiding inside, your shopping in privacy also saves you time—and usually money—since it's easy to compare prices on the Web.

Of course, whatever you order online has to get from somewhere to somewhere else—so how can you be sure that with all the air freight and diesel-spewing delivery trucks and warehouse boxes and packing peanuts you're still coming out ahead eco-wise? We've been there and worried about it too. But here are the good green reasons we learned from one of our all-time favorite green resources, www.idealbite.com, about why shopping online might be your best bet:

1. You can send gifts straight to the giftee, to avoid double shipping.

2. Despite their size, e-commerce warehouses use one-sixteenth of the energy used to operate retail stores.

3. Even overnight air shipping uses 40 percent less fuel than the average car trip to the store. Who knew? Ground shipping is still six times more energy efficient than air, so if you order ahead of time and exercise patience, you'll really shop guilt-free!

So go ahead and shop in the cozy comfort of your own room! But if you're going to be running errands soon, think it through. It may be best to pick up what you need while already out and about.

Now let's take a look at some of your favorite shopping categories and help you figure out how to make the greenest choices in each one.

jewelry: gilding without guilt

Gold

There's such hot-looking jewelry out there, and it can be so much fun to wear. But if you're into gold, it might surprise you to know that thousands of gallons of water are used to make even a small piece of gold jewelry. *Thousands of gallons.* Why? Because the gold in that ring or earring you're wearing was probably extracted from the ore with cyanide—a poisonous chemical that damages the brain and heart (and is even a potential ingredient for chemical terrorism). Of course, you don't want cyanide next to your skin, so it has to be rinsed off with lots and lots of water.

Then, to get the gold to even look like a ring or earring it must be cast, stripped, cleaned, and plated—and again thoroughly rinsed between each step, according to a California EPA report called Wastewater Produced in Jewelry Manufacturing. That's a pretty good title for the report, by the way, because that's exactly what's left: dirty, corrosive wastewater full of dissolved metals and cyanide.

And then there's the waste generated from the gold mines to take into account. According to Oxfam America, a single 18-karat gold ring can generate nearly twenty tons of mine waste! That waste often ends up getting dumped near rivers or streams, not only carrying the poisons downstream, but clogging those waterways and killing fish and destroying surrounding ecosystems. Does your ring or earring suddenly feel heavier?

Inexpensive jewelry can be problematic too, most significantly with the potential for a high lead count. After testing pieces of inexpensive jewelry from local stores, Ashland University chemistry students found that most of them "vastly exceeded the U.S. Consumer Product Safety Commission (CPSC) guidelines of a maximum lead content of 0.06 percent by weight."

It seemed like 2007 was the year of "lead poisoning." You couldn't turn on the news without hearing about another toy recall. According to the Coalition to End Childhood Lead Poisoning, lead is also in children's jewelry, with millions of pieces being recalled by the CPSC—much of it costume jewelry or sold in discount stores.

Silver looks beautiful around your neck, but did you know that for centuries people used it to fight germs? Until antibiotics replaced it, silver was a key ingredient in antimicrobial medicines. Today it's used instead of chlorine to sanitize swimming pools. NASA even uses silver to purify water in the space shuttle!

Diamonds—a Girl's Best Friend?

If you're into diamonds, look for "conflict-free" diamonds. Remember the movie *Blood Diamond* starring Leonardo DiCaprio? As that film showed, "conflict diamonds" have been responsible for funding civil wars in Africa and for killing literally millions of people.

Conflict-free diamonds, on the other hand, come from ethically and environmentally responsible sources, free of any violence or human rights abuses. They're also easier on the environment. A quick search at www.idealbite.com will give you a handful of retailers of both jewelry and diamonds to oogle over.

When you do a search online for any kind of green jewelry makers, try using words such as: "certified green gold" or platinum, or look for jewelry that's guaranteed to be sustainably mined or fairly traded.

If you want to buy a quality piece of jewelry, another great option is to check out your local resale shop or antiques store. Vintage jewels can be prettier, better made, and less expensive than newer pieces. And these hot collectibles ease stress on natural systems.

Of course, you can always make jewelry of your own—out of eco-friendly beads! Ancient Egyptians loved jewelry, creating solid glass beads as far back as 4000 B.C. and clay beads as early as 12,000 B.C. Around the world beads have held a spiritual/magical mystique. The English word "bead" derived from the Old English meaning "to pray." The Egyptian hieroglyph for "bead" is the same as for "luck." Also look for beads made of natural fiber, ceramic, and other sustainable treasures with which to adorn your green self.

the green wrinkle in clothes

Cotton

Who doesn't like to snuggle into a cozy sweatshirt on a cold winter's morning, or wear that comfy worn T-shirt until it begs to be washed, or fall asleep on cotton flannel sheets in the wintertime? Do you ever think, *Ah, cotton. A natural fiber. It's so green!* We hear you, but all cotton is not green, as it turns out. In fact, regular conventionally grown cotton, which accounts for only 3 percent of the world's farmland, uses about 25 percent of the world's chemical pesticides! In the United States alone a quarter of all pesticides used are for growing cotton. According to *The Rough Guide to Shopping with a Conscience* by Duncan Clark and Richie Unterberger, more than half of the cotton on sale now is estimated to be genetically engineered (GE).

The organic cotton industry, in contrast, doesn't use any pesticides, herbicides, or chemicals in the growing or processing of its fiber—making it our all-time favorite clothing choice. Its production uses less fuel and emits fewer greenhouse gases than conventional cotton production. (Now, of course we could talk about the fuels used to power the machines that spin the threads, knit and weave the fabrics, and transport them to the consumer—you—but who's counting?) Cotton is one of the most popular, widely traded products on the planet—so do your best to make the switch to organic whenever possible.

Hemp

Clothing, hats, bags, and other accessories made of hemp are another terrific option. As we discussed in Chapter One, hemp is also a fantastic fiber, requiring few pesticides or fertilizers, and it's fast-growing and drought tolerant. When hemp clothing first appeared on the scene, it was scratchy and unappealing. Today's generation of hemp has lost that hippie-dippie feeling and is smooth, soft, and stylish, with designers such as Calvin Klein, Ralph Lauren, and Giorgio Armani already introducing collections Studies have shown that hemp clothing keeps wearers cooler than cotton; hemp even appears to be microbe-resistant. Feasibility studies are under way to see if hemp is a viable option for the uniforms for Canada's 2010 Olympic team.

Bamboo

People have been embracing bamboo like crazy recently because it's even softer than the softest cotton! And it's renewable. The plant—really a type of grass, actually—doesn't have to die when it's harvested. It just gets cut back so that the roots (and earth) stay intact. Much like hemp, it's sort of magical and can grow up to twenty-four inches per day—think of it like Jack's bean stalk! Also like hemp, it requires almost no pesticides and can grow nearly anywhere. Bamboo has been the main building material in Asia for eons. It's strong and looks like wood. In fact, it's the flooring for our kitchen in Los Angeles, and it's gorg!

In comparison to organic cotton, however, bamboo has a way to go in environmental friendliness. While its growth doesn't hurt ecosystems, processing the fiber for clothes is not as pure a process. This will be something to watch in the coming years as some producers are getting hip to the watchdogs and are cleaning up their acts.

Leather

Wondering if there's such a thing as green leather? If you tan hides the Native American way, using the animal's brains or eggs, it can be. Tosh has a friend who once lugged home a road-kill deer and tanned it in his backyard (no kidding), and believe us, it was a labor-intensive process! Most leather, however, isn't eco-friendly. Aside from the obvious drawback— that it comes from animals and raises an animal's slaughterhouse value—the processing of leather is a chemical-laden affair that includes carcinogenic toxins. Almost twenty thousand gallons of water are required to process one ton of rawhide! Scientists in India have developed a greener tanning process that cuts the chemicals used by 82 percent and has energy savings of 40 percent, but it's not widely commercially available yet. Thankfully, there are leather alternatives. Linda's oldest and most worn-in fave pair of cowgirl boots are made without animal products, as are her ski chalet UGG boot look-alikes. You'd never know. Which proves that you don't have to give up style or comfort when you shop around. Go to www.peta.org for links to nonleather suppliers.

Stella McCartney looked to her mom, Linda McCartney, who taught her about vegetarianism. Now as a designer she refuses to use animal skins and furs and has made a niche for herself with her sustainable designs. It's fun to want to look like (and look up to) the beautiful fashion models, both male and female, but how about looking up to (and supporting with your green dollars) those people like Stella who are all about a new, fresh approach to green fashion?

the green sporting life

Playing sports is great for your health, but there's still an environmental impact from the manufacturing and disposal of all those clothes, shoes, and equipment. A typical family amasses a mountain of often barely used equipment and uniforms. Some enterprising towns organize free swaps where families can exchange outgrown stuff for the next size up or simply donate to kids less fortunate. Think of gathering up donations from your team at the end of the season so the coach can give them to shelters (or those forgetful teens who show up for game day without suiting up).

One World Running, www.oneworldrunning.com, will send still-wearable shoes to athletes who need them in Africa, Latin America, and Haiti.

Many large companies—Nike, Patagonia, and Timberland—are trying to use more organic cotton, solar and wind energy, and so forth, to produce greener athletic shoes. Nike is even using "gasification" at their Dominican Republic plant, which is a way to turn into gas leftover "waste leather" and use it as fuel.

green beauty is skin deep

Of course you're aware that most beauty products are filled with chemicals. But here's something you probably don't think about: You shampoo and condition your hair and soap up in the shower, where the hot steam carries a lot of those chemicals straight into your lungs. That's why it pays to read the labels to see if you know what you're putting on your hair, face, and body. Something else to think about: If your boyfriend kisses you on the cheek, what's ending up on his lips?

Toxic Lipsticks and Glosses

Want to hear something crazy? The average woman swallows six pounds of lipstick within her lifetime! We'd never ask you to go cold turkey on lip glosses and or lip balms—but we suggest you learn to check the labels.

A 2006 article in *Ms.* magazine explains that some of the chemicals in popular cosmetics—phthalates, formaldehyde, petroleum, parabens, benzene, and lead—have been linked to breast cancer, endometriosis, reproductive disorders, birth defects, and developmental disabilities in children. Another study, this one by the National Institute for Occupational Safety and Health, lists as toxic 884 chemicals used by the cosmetics industry. And yet the FDA makes cosmetics companies responsible for their own product safety testing. Why is that? Because the beauty and cosmetics industry in the United States is not regulated by the Food and Drug Administration (FDA). Even though traces of toxins can be found in your tissues and organs (entering your system through your largest organ—your skin) after using popular cosmetics brands, they're not individually safety approved before going on sale.

Many of the substances sold in cosmetics here at home are now illegal in Europe, and for good reason. Women are particularly at risk since the female body is more susceptible to certain environmental chemicals because of a greater percentage of body fat, which absorbs and stores these toxins. Dibutyl phthalate, commonly found in nail polish and as a scent in hair sprays and deodorants, has been banned because it's linked to cancer. So too are artificial colors such as blue 1, green 3, or FD&C pigments, also believed to be carcinogenic.

Companies like the Body Shop, Burt's Bees, and Aubrey Organics have signed the Compact for Safe Cosmetics agreement, initiated by international pressure to discontinue the use of known toxic ingredients. So you might want to start with those companies when looking for your next beauty creams, lotions, or potions.

Because cosmetics companies are not required to label ingredients (how absurd is that?) and the FDA doesn't test them, you the consumer have got to do your homework. Fortunately, Governor Arnold Schwarzenegger recently signed the California Safe Cosmetics Act into law to take effect in 2007, requiring that manufacturers come clean about ingredients and their potential dangers. California is leading the way with this legislation; and the hope is that this kind of watchdog law will catch on in the rest of the country.

Also look for cosmetics labeled cruelty-free, which means no testing on live animals (typically meaning lab animals such as dogs, cats, monkeys, and rabbits), who can't say no.

Beauty from the Kitchen

Before spending your green dough, think about what you might find in your own natural and healthy kitchen. If you talk to your grandmother or great-grandmother, she might remember a time when homemade beauty remedies were the norm. The following are a few of Linda's favorite home remedies (of course Tosh would *never* have tried any of these):

- Oatmeal naturally exfoliates your skin. Mix with water, lightly cook, and scrub away!

- Lie down with avacado slices under each eye and rest for fifteen to twenty minutes to relieve puffiness.

- Soak week nails in warm extra virgin olive oil for five minutes to strengthen them.

- Whiten your teeth with equal parts sea salt and baking soda. (Okay, Tosh admits he loves this one!)

- Want to try the world's best facial mask? Take one organic free-range egg white, whip for ten seconds with a fork in a bowl with one half of a tablespoon of honey. Apply to your clean, dry face and then rinse after fifteen minutes.

DEADLY BEAUTY

Well into the nineteenth century, ladies achieved a prized pale complexion by applying carbonate, hydroxide, and lead oxide to their faces, which sometimes caused muscle paralysis and even death. They also used poisonous lead and antimony as eye shadow and used eyedrops made of deadly nightshade to dilate their pupils to look more alluring.

Nail Polish

Skin Deep, an interactive product safety database, says that nail polish is a big concern in terms of potential serious health effects. Many greener lines are springing up, which is good news because chemicals like formaldehyde, toluene, and dibutyl phthalate (DBP), and VOCs, used in many larger brands should be avoided because of their toxicity levels.

Does that mean you have to give up your mani-pedis? Hardly! Linda was first introduced to toxin-free nail salons by her buddy Dayna Devon. Their products are low on odor and poisons but high on shine! Ask your local salon which eco-friendly brands they use, and if they don't carry any just yet, suggest that they do. Until that time, how about bringing your own bottles with you? Aside from the Varnish brand, Linda recommends PeaceKeeper and WaterColors nail enamels. Ask the clerk at your local health food store what names he or she recommends.

Perfume

The word "fragrance" on a label can indicate the presence of up to four thousand separate ingredients, many toxic or carcinogenic. Some of the symptoms reported to the FDA relating to fragrances include headaches, dizziness, allergic rashes, skin discoloration, violent coughing and vomiting, and skin irritation. The use of fragrances can affect the central nervous system and can cause depression, hyperactivity, and irritability. Use natural organic oils whenever possible instead. They smell naturally delicious and won't cause you or anyone else harm.

Antiperspirant

No one wants sweaty armpits. People have been trying to avoid them for ages—the Victorians sponged their armpits with sulphuric acid, risking burns because they believed it helped underarms stay dry. You may have heard the rumor that deodorants are potentially harmful to your health, and it makes sense if you stop and think about it. After all, for most of us there's hardly a sweatier place on our body than our armpits, and that's the point—to cleanse toxins through our perspiration. But take a second to think about what happens if you block the pores to this area, inhibiting their normal sweating function. Those toxins can't flush out of your system as easily, right?

Moreover, most commercial brands of antiperspirants and deodorants contain ingredients like aluminum chlorohydrate or aluminum zirconium. Aluminum, as you may know, has been linked to Alzheimer's Disease and breast cancer and is easily absorbed by the body. Once absorbed, the molecules ionize and form free radicals that pass readily across cell membranes for absorption by the liver, kidney, brain, cartilage, and even the bone marrow. (We find our favorite aluminum-free brands, especially the Crystal Body Deodorant brand, at any major health food store.)

For more information, check out the Teens for Safe Cosmetics campaign at www.searchforthecause.org.

How Can You Apply the Five Rs When It Comes to Beauty Products?

First let's think about reuse and recycle. Our friend Brenda was addicted to blue eye shadow and didn't realize how many she owned until she did a drawer inventory. A neighbor, Sarah, had purchased seven bronzers (and didn't love any of them) before it occurred to her to spend more time at the store with testers before just throwing more money at yet another brand. (If the fear of running into friends makes you race through the shopping process, try shopping at a store in a different neighborhood.)

Changing all the time is cool, but it's also cool to find your signature. Another friend, Dena, started wearing sparkles on her cheeks at thirteen years old, and today at twenty-one she still wears them. That's her signature. She knows who she is and what she likes, and therefore doesn't spend a lot of money buying new products trying to find a new signature.

Of course, if you want to experiment, try new things, or figure out what you like, do it all in the context of "rethink." Ask yourself, "If I'm going to buy this new eye shadow, will I commit to using it for the next three months?" Can you commit right now to keeping the next pair of jeans you purchase in your wardrobe for x amount of months? If you can't commit to it right then and there, that's how you know you're probably going to waste your purchase.

What if you only want something for one big event—a prom, sweet sixteen, or a *Quinceañera*? Do you really need to buy it, or can you rent or trade or make do with what you have? We all want that special thing for a big event. If you know you're going to wear that prom dress only once, find a place where you can resell it or give it away. Not only resale shops but also charities now find prom dresses for people who can't afford them.

the karma of green shopping

Just as when you're buying organic produce, sometimes the greener choice will cost more when you're shopping. Again, think of the green karma you'll be earning. And since you probably can't vote yet, this is perhaps the best way for you to really make your voice heard. If you like a product, support that product—and "vote" for it by buying it. That kind of consumer power only grows.

It can be harder to find cruelty-free products, and sometimes you'll want to take the easier route of buying a regular product. Or maybe you don't want to give up leather but feel bad about the stress on animals and the environment. Animal communicator and bestselling author Amelia Kinkade in her book *Straight from the Horse's*

Mouth: How to Talk to Animals and Get Answers gives us a new, greener way to view the karma of animal testing and products made from animals.

> *Sometimes the best way to get your prayers answered is to answer the prayers of others. If you have conflicts about your behavior, as we all do, tithing is a great way to balance the scales. If you feel lousy about some hypocrisy in your diet, tithe to a charity like the National Anti-Vivisection Society, People for the Ethical Treatment of Animals, the ARK Trust, Friends of Animals, the Gorilla Foundation, or the National Humane Society. If you have whittled the furry animals out of your diet, but you still eat feathered ones, volunteer once a week at your local wildlife rehabilitation center. If you feel guilty about the leather trim on your new purse, volunteer to walk the dogs at your local no-kill shelter. The dogs will love you for it.*
>
> *We all suffer now in our day-to-day lives just by our inability to commune with our furry friends. Only if we cherish and protect them can they bring the endless joy they want to bring us. Everything is a choice. We have the power to direct or debilitate whole industries.*

Tosh loves shopping; maybe you can relate. But he's learning to be more creative when the easier choice would be to simply run out and buy something. That's the best thing about going green—it really makes you think about fun, interesting ways to do something better. For instance, what about combining shopping *and* helping the earth? Tosh found a way to meld the two last

Mother's Day, when he couldn't figure out what to buy Linda.

Usually he'd just go to the mall to buy something he'd heard her say she wanted. Then last year he decided to do something different, something memorable. He was out in the yard doing one of his chores—watering the fruit trees—and he got an idea. He finished up, snuck up into his room, and grabbed some recycled printer paper to put his idea down on a homemade card. He wrote "Universal Gift Card" on the front of the card and drew a funky tree underneath, with the words "Save the World = Linda Sivertsen." He slid a hundred-dollar bill in there and gave it to Linda on Mother's Day morning. She cried, of course. "What time can we go to your favorite nursery?" he asked. She couldn't believe he'd thought of her favorite place.

Tosh had just gotten his license and drove them both across town to Greens. They filled up the car with a ton of plants and a cool little ceramic dog she liked, and they spent the rest of the day digging and planting. He never thought he'd want to do this for a whole Sunday, but it was one of the best days Linda and Tosh have ever spent together. Not long after, she came in with a bowl full of lettuce from their Mother's Day plant-a-thon, and Tosh realized that the gift keeps giving. He's trying to figure out how he can do this for every holiday cuz that was easy, fun, memorable, and green!

For a truly different kind of "shopping," what about the kind that doesn't use any money at all? . . .

the **ultimate** swapster:
AN INTERVIEW WITH JON BOOTH

A two-hundred-dollar double bass drum pedal. A practically new computer monitor. A shiny pair of men's formal tuxedo shoes. These are just a few of the things that Jon Booth, a senior at White Plains High School in White Plains, New York, has gotten for nothing since he discovered his first "Really Really Free Market" while wandering around New York City. He loved the idea so much that he's been hosting his own in his hometown since the summer of 2007.

When Jon says "really, really free," he means it. "There's no requirement to bring anything," he says. "It's not like a swap, where you have to exchange. The point is that it's a gift economy; people who don't have stuff can get stuff they need." You simply show up and take whatever you like. Period. How cool is that?

Really Really Free Markets (also called "Freemeets") are also a great way to get rid of stuff you don't need or use—old clothes, books, toys, and household goods. At his last market Jon scooped up a box of old test-prep books and dropped them off at his high school's guidance office. "After you take the SAT or AP, you don't need those things anymore, and they're expensive," he says.

Want to start your own? First pick a location. "Choose a public place where lots of people walk by," Jon advises. Once, Jon e-mailed a local church and asked if he could use the front lawn. "Great!" said the pastor. Next do as much promotion as possible. "There will always be lots more people who'd love to go if they knew about it." It's worth the effort, Jon believes. "The markets are always a lot of fun. It's a good way to get people together to do something good and to recycle what they have to people who need it."

For more information, contact www.freegan.info. Other free sites include www.freecycle.org and the free section of your local craigslist.

HANGING OUT
GREEN

It's summer vacation and you're chillin' around the house playing video games with your friends. It's been a few hours now and it hits you that your air conditioner and fan are both blowing over your head. You're suddenly inspired, thinking *I bet I really don't need both of these* as you stand up to turn off the fan. You look around and notice that your friends are all bleary-eyed from the games, and you suggest an alternative.

"Want to go throw the football around?" Blank stares. But you press on. "Come on. Then we'll walk to get some food." A rumble of life starts to murmur around you and you've just successfully shifted a pattern. Maybe this is what Dad was talking about when he droned on and on about the days "before" video games—the days when teens actually spent hours, days even, *outside*!

This chapter asks how you can have fun doing things that don't waste resources or put undue stress on fragile ecosystems. Even better, we'll take a look at things that actually *contribute* to the environment—leaving the planet better than when you found it. Is that really possible? Read on.

So let's start with one of the most important things in life . . . music! You're a music freak? Funny coincidence—we're music freaks too! But do you ever wonder if your listening habits put further stress on Mama Earth? Sorry to say but yes, there's an impact. So, what to do? Do you have to go cold turkey and sing yourself to sleep? *Oh no.* Hopefully our homework here will give you some answers.

the magic of technology

Downloading music feels like the ultimate green experience. You're sitting at your desk, and with a few keystrokes you're listening to the artist of your choice without so much as driving an inch or unwrapping a thing! It feels like magic, and satisfies your need for speed.

If you're like Tosh, the ease of downloading ensures that you've got a lot of music at your disposal, and your iPod or MP3 player sometimes feels like an extension of your body—playing the accompanying soundtrack of your life from morning until night, with you as the ultimate DJ. No matter what your mood, the sounds coming from your player reflect it—from full-on hyper mode to happily cruising along to totally mellowed out. It's fun and can make your day feel so much richer and more creative.

With all of this music playing, it's understandable that you're going to wear out these players from time to time, and you've probably got your fair share of scratched and broken CDs lying around too. In fact, with the explosion of affordable technology, especially when it comes to cell phones and computers, you probably have several old or broken items that need to be disposed of, if you only knew where! Until very recently most of us just threw them into the trash. But there is a greener way.

What's Technotrash?

"Technotrash" encompasses a lot of things, including: CDs, DVDs, and diskettes (and their cases), video and audio tapes (and their cases), inkjet and toner cartridges, cell phones, pagers and PDAs, cords, cables, mice, printed circuit boards, computers, monitors, hard drives, zip and Jaz drives, rechargeable batteries and their chargers, MP3 players, iPods, digital cameras, handheld games, and so on. Got all that? Phew! Fortunately, for a small fee GreenDisk (www.greendisk.com) and Ecodisk (www.ecodisk.com) will take it all off your hands, destroy the data, and recycle the rest. That is, they'll trash your technotrash. They'll even pick it up at your house or send you a mailer so you can pop it into the mail.

You can also log on to www.earth911.org to find out more about recycling these items in your area. Entering your zip code will send you straight to local resources.

E-waste

You spend a small fortune on the latest gadget, but you've barely left the store and your newfangled thingamajig's suddenly upgraded with a newer version. Sure, the next time you blink, your computer, MP3 player, and DVD player will have morphed into sleeker, faster, hotter versions—but oh well! Mounds of these "old" relics, often in perfectly good condition, become electronic waste, or e-waste—about 1.5 billion pounds a year. Toxic metals, anyone? Let's stop the madness! Don't buy so quickly. When you're done, donate. Or find a legitimate recycler.

What's the Difference Between Technotrash and E-waste?

While the two terms are sometimes used interchangably, e-waste often refers to computer waste—both hardware and software. If a company has an e-waste problem, they need a way to safely dispose of their computers or wipe the hard drives clean of sensitive data so the computers can be passed along to schools and other organizations who can give them new life. But some people dub *any* broken or unwanted electrical or electronic appliance e-waste (which could include your old toaster or cell phone). According to Wikipedia, if you can recycle your e-waste, it's a commodity, but if it can't be reused, it's, well, true e-waste, since many components are toxic and nonbiodegradable.

Perhaps more important than technicalities is how fast this waste accumulates! Wrap your mind around this: Americans retire 426,000 cell phones a day (with only one in ten being recycled). Whether you call it e-waste or technotrash doesn't really matter. What does matter is that all this heavy metal toxic junk is becoming a problem. It's more important than ever to dispose of things safely, since technology seems to move faster than the speed of light.

With all of this talk about trash and waste, let's investigate the best way to reduce your impact when buying music.

download this?

According to the National Wildlife Federation's online Green Consumer column, *millions* of boxes of software CDs end up in landfills and incinerators. In the next five years some estimates say that'll amount to more than ten *billion* CDs and DVDs becoming waste, when virtually *all* of them could be recycled or gifted to someone who'd value them.

CDs and DVDs

If you've ever stopped to really look at a plastic CD case—"jewel case"—you know it's made from high-quality heavy plastic. Then there's the CD itself, also made of plastic—called polycarbonate. And the liner notes—those are made of paper, which may or may not be recycled. Of course, if you take this little product and break down its life cycle *before* it arrives in stores, you'll see that there was a whole lot of processing and distribution involved behind the scenes. Think about all of those construction and decorating materials used for the building where you're buying these rockin' tunes, and all that lighting, heating, and cooling—that's mounds of *stuff* that's all part of the machine surrounding the sales of your little CD. It's sort of mind-boggling when you begin traveling down this path, don't you think?

Our friends at www.treehugger.com tell us that a kilogram of greenhouse gases is generated for each CD produced, packaged, and delivered (roughly half of the gases coming from production and half from transportation). Remember our black balloon example from Chapter Three? That's nearly eighteen balloons floating straight out of your computer for each CD in existence! Ouch.

So downloading seems like the greenest option. But is it really as green as it seems? Well, that all depends. Downloading music does save energy compared with buying it in the store, even if you own the most non-eco-friendly MP3 players and the like. In an article in the *Guardian* in October 2006 called "Is It OK . . . to Use an MP3 Player?" writer Leo Hickman looked at all the angles and discovered that downloading, although hardly a zero-impact practice (when you factor in the energy expended for the players and the physical infrastructure for downloading), is still at a clear advantage over buying CDs in stores.

However, there's a big BUT lurking in this equation. Downloading tunes saves energy over store-bought music every time . . . unless and *until* you burn a CD of that music at home. Then the numbers skew the other way—becoming nearly three times as wasteful in terms of resources as buying the original music on a CD at a mall or superstore! Ugh. So, now what? Our advice is to take a moment to rethink before you burn CDs for your car, your portable CD player, and your BFFs. We all love sharing files with our friends and family (when legal, of course), but what about this idea: Your friend brings his or her iPod or computer over to your house, you hook your system up to their system with a USB cord, and all the file sharing you need is done in a snap—skipping every one of the previous wasteful steps altogether!

Ah. It feels greener around here already.

better safe than sorry!

Backing Up Your Data

Maybe you've learned the hard way how important it can be to back up your favorite songs, photos, or documents. Linda has run several laptops into early graves, literally overusing them until they smoked and crashed before her eyes. She thus became backup-obsessed, burning CDs as though her life depended on it. Eventually she found rewritable compact discs, which she still uses occasionally, saving on waste. But her big hallelujah breakthrough moment came when she signed up for an online data storage system through the Apple store where she bought her Mac laptop, which now daily backs up all of her writing files, including her rambling e-mail folders. This cut Linda's need for CDs by 95 percent. Props for technology!

Check out www.carbonite.com and www.flipdrive. com for other online data storage companies. They'll store *all* of your stuff—files, photos, music, favorite Internet sites—with plans starting at less than five dollars per month. (FlipDrive even has a free account that gives you twenty-five megabytes of storage!) Most companies have a fifteen-to-thirty-day risk-free trial, and some don't even require a credit card for you to try them out.

Once you sign on, you're saving the earth from CD technotrash and sleeping better because you don't have to worry about crashes and viruses. But there are some other things about online storage that are pretty cool: You can access your files instantly from any computer on the planet, and you can share files easily with friends, no matter what the size. Worried about privacy? Most services say that your files are encrypted before they even leave your computer. And some companies, like FlipDrive, boast that they're green while providing this green service. As a company they control sources of energy coming into the office, carefully select office supplies, and manage waste production. You can call and quiz them yourself before deciding which company to choose, but doesn't this sound better than dealing with external hard drives (that can be hacked into) and storing tons of CDs?

If you're like us and need to buy CDs once in a while, remember to donate them to friends, churches, libraries, schools, or charities once you're finished with them, or send them to one of the companies that safely disposes of them.

Okay, this is all cool and definitely fits under our reuse and recycle categories. But in keeping with looking at some of the other Rs we talked about in Chapter One, what about refusing some of this stuff in the first place? What about not ever buying those CDs and DVDs at all? In that case, get back to downloading, you savvy green teen!

> Waste adds up! According to Project KOPEG (Keep Our Planet Earth Green, www.projectkopeg.com), Americans consume 1,370,000 ink cartridges every single day! Next time you think you've got to make a copy of those silly e-mails between you and your BFF, maybe wait a day to see if you still find them riveting.

So now that you've got all that great music downloaded, and you've lined up some fab resources to handle your technotrash and e-waste, it's time to have a party for your friends, wouldn't you say? How's about a greener twist on the old standard get-together?

partying green

To kick off your green-themed party (no, we're not talking politics!), use e-vites or e-card invitations, but not those cutesy ones that make you gag. Try wowing your friends instead with a colorful e-card from Conservation International at www.conservation.org. They've got over a dozen cards that prove that conservation is beautiful. And, of course, e-vites save paper. (We use them so much now that sometimes we forget about all those stamps, envelopes, and card stock that no longer clog the system.) But if you really want paper invites, you can trust the Sierra Club to provide cards printed with soy-based ink on recycled paper, or look for non-tree fiber alternatives.

THE INTERNET IS GREEN

Finally, some very good green news! A 2007 report by the American Consumer Institute says that the Internet will be responsible for saving the world almost one *billion* tons of carbon over the next ten years. This is a result of the print media—newspapers and magazines—going ever more digital, e-commerce reducing our emissions by two hundred million tons, and telecommuting and teleconferencing saving even more.

When your guests come over, try serving healthy drinks—like homemade lemonade and freshly brewed organic free-trade iced tea. If a party without sodas is simply not going to happen at your place, try a health food store brand instead, or check to see if your favorite brand comes in the more eco-friendly glass bottles. Some offer cash refunds too. In bypassing landfills altogether by encouraging people to return their bottles to the place of purchase, this "closed-loop system"—the three chasing arrows—is the ideal. If that's not how you roll, pick up the large plastic bottles instead of those individual cans, pour each drink into a real glass for your guests, and be sure to toss those bottles into the recycle bin. Your friends may not know that their bottles will become polyester fiber for carpets, sleeping bags, and fleece clothing once recycled, but maybe there's a way to slip that interesting tidbit of information into the topic of conversation without sounding preachy?

As for plates and utensils, try using the washable stuff. You know, the kind you don't throw away at the end of the day and send to overburdened landfills. That'll leave you less to recycle after everyone leaves, and more to feel proud of. Again, if that's just not going to happen, try to remember to put out a recycling bin or two and keep the cans and recyclables separate from the real trash. Who knows . . . you might just earn a little street cred, and you might interest your guests with a demonstration of how their leftover pasta salad or popcorn goes into your handy countertop composter and turns to real-life earth. Tosh was mesmerized when his buddy in upstate New York demonstrated this for him, forever changing his view of what constitutes real trash.

If you're having trouble visualizing what a green-themed party looks like, here are a few options to get you thinking.

Extreme Room Makeover Party

What about helping out a friend by having a party to help him set up his college dorm room or his first apartment—or even just to redo his tired old bedroom? Jump into some old clothes that you don't mind getting eco-friendly paint on, and show your buddy that today it's all about him and updating his digs. The Junk Brothers—Steve and Jim Kelley of HGTV—literally find pieces of discarded junk (sinks, cupboards, pieces of cars), take them back to their workshop, and turn them into cool-looking pieces of furniture. What could you create by putting your heads together? You don't have to think practical. Think fun. Think art! Of course, your favorite tunes are blasting while those organic snacks, drinks, and deserts await—a reward for time well spent.

Found Art Party

For this party you get to combine cleaning up the neighborhood *and* making art. You and your friends can go out scouting—preferably on trash day—where you might find just the right thing on the curb. You can also visit a thrift/charity store for worthy items. Just be sure to clean things before lugging them into your house to avoid unwanted pests. (And watch out for splinters and rough edges!) Oh, and carting home a neighbor's treasures—like their potted plants or porch furniture—is a no no! LOL! Bring your loot back to the party house, and with whatever you want—eco-paints, glues, papers, stuff you've found in your closets, jewelry boxes, pantries, and drawers—make sculptures, paintings, or wall hangings. Did you find an oddly shaped scrap of wood? Use it as a canvas and paint a painting on it. An old mailbox? Paint it with bright colors and mount it in the kitchen for outgoing mail. A weather-beaten ceramic pot? Give it a fresh look by gluing seashells to the outside. You get the idea—anything goes. (Ever see the "Get Fuzzy" comic strip when Bucky the cat breaks everything in the house, glues it together, paints it gold leaf, and calls it art? That's kind of what we're talking about here, only without the air of destruction.) Next, invite more friends to the Found-Object Art Show and sell the art so that you can contribute your green cash to a local green cause. Maybe your high school campus is in desperate need of some greenery? Get creative—green creative!

T-shirt Party

For a cool coed party idea, have your friends "make over" an old T-shirt they no longer wear because they're tired of it, it's stained, or it's too big or too small. Then get out those clippers and recut them into something new. There are all sorts of ideas and T-shirt makeover books. (Our favorite is *Closet Control* by Barbra Horowitz—with an accompanying video that will teach you how to redo your whole closet if you're so brave.) Make them, swap them, trade them before you make them over; there are limitless possibilities. You can make them as gifts, or give your dog a new outfit.

If you're partied out and you want a change of scenery, what's next? Get out and do some eco-bonding.

Save a Beach

Do you live on or near a coastline? There are lots of clubs and organizations devoted to cleaning up the ecosystems surrounding beaches, lakes, and waterways. Try calling your city's lifeguard department (sometimes listed under "Parks and Recreation") and ask if they can put you in touch with local groups with names like Save the Ocean (Beach, Bay) or Save the Seals—or other groups of people in your town who are working to protect the environment. Sometimes nonprofits for surfing are a good place to start since the future of their fun depends on a safe and healthy beach!

green surfing:

AN INTERVIEW WITH SAMSON ANDERSON-MAGAZINO

Surf's up and Samson's up early to catch a few waves on another sparkling Santa Barbara morning. Taking in the crisp air and wading in the cool ocean water, he sniffs and looks down as raw sewage floats by. Unfortunately for eighteen-year-old Samson Anderson-Magazino, a Santa Barbara, California, local, this sight is not uncommon.

Samson says much of the sewage comes from backed-up septic tanks of nearby upscale homes that overflow during rainy weather and dump into the ocean. "It's not pleasant," says Magazino. "It's even gotten me sick—strep throat and fevers."

Magazino, a student at Santa Barbara City College, says that as a surfer he's spent a lot of time in the water and that it has made him acutely aware of ocean pollution. This awareness has driven him to join Heal the Ocean, a local environmental group that works to locate the source of ocean pollution and suggest practical solutions.

One practical answer Magazino has for improving ocean pollution is reminding everyone that "whatever you toss into the street or pour down the drain today you might be swimming in tomorrow." Litter and chemicals, he explains, don't just disappear. "All that junk gets washed into creeks and rivers and eventually makes its way into the ocean." The solution? "Simple," he says. "We have to stop using our oceans as Dumpsters."

One of Magazino's favorite Heal the Ocean fund-raising events has been the annual surf-a-thon, where sponsored surfers raise money for the organization by surfing the most waves they can in a designated period of time. "In our last surf-a-thon we raised fifteen hundred dollars. That's pretty cool for just having fun and surfing."

We totally agree, Samson!

green gardening

Start an Organic Vegetable Garden

Maybe we can tempt you with the mouthwatering promise
of tasty organic vegetables for your summer barbeque.
Find a plot of land you and your friends can share—often
there are public ones available—or find a spot in your backyard
with a lot of sun. It's amazing how many things you can grow
in just a few feet of earth—zucchinis, tomatoes, cucumbers,
and bell peppers sprout like weeds! Till the soil with your
friends, plant the veggies, gather together to water and weed,
and then watch the vegetables mature before grilling veggie
kebobs on the propane barbeque for everyone. Mmm . . . delish!

Volunteer at an Already-Established Public Garden

Some public parks and botanical gardens need extra help to
keep these beautiful public spaces in tip-top shape. Are there
any such green masterpieces near you? If you're not sure or
don't think this sounds like your deal, we urge you to check it
out before deciding against it. One of Tosh's favorite places
on earth is the Huntington Botanical Gardens in Pasadena,
California. He could spend half a day in the cactus section
alone! And don't even think of rushing him through the sky-
high bamboo jungle near the tea garden where Tom Cruise shot
parts of *The Last Samurai.* Even as an eighteen-year-old, Tosh is
still compelled to get lost amidst
the massive stalks, just as he did as a little boy. (And yes, ahem,
we're aware you're not supposed to walk in there.) Seriously,
think about it—If you've ever visited a nursery and noticed
feeling immediately relaxed and suddenly hopeful, that's

Mother Nature working her magic on your heart and soul. And for those of us who live in cities, we need this connection more than we know. See if there's a nearby volunteer program and check it out sooner rather than later.

Now that we've established that nature is a great place to hang out, could it be time for a little hike in the woods?

camp lightly

When Linda was a kid, her parents frequently took her hiking through the forests of Northern California. When they weren't visiting or actually setting up camp, she was sent to an amazing wilderness summer camp high in the Sierras. Because of this experience and because of the huge pines and redwoods in the yard of her childhood home, Linda came to think of trees as a sort of second skin. In all of her traipsing through the woods, she never once remembers seeing a piece of trash where it didn't belong. Rocks painted with graffiti? Never! But nowadays it's different, isn't it? The world has changed. The sad fact is that there are a lot of yahoos pitching tents out there and littering the landscape. If the ancient monuments and statues of Rome could be spoiled with graffiti (and they are—ugh), our living monuments aren't so fortunate as to get a hall pass.

But even though some people think that the planet's a giant trash can and treat national monuments like scratch pads, there are still wondrous places that we can enjoy while having a minimal impact on the environment. Camping can and *should* be eco-friendly. If the very term "camping" conjures up images for you of walking with butterflies flitting around your head and of hearing the song of crickets at night while witnessing deer grazing on tall grasses from the glow of your campfire, hold on to that image! You're probably wondering why we aren't telling you to stay home and give nature a break. Because, again, nature heals us. We need it. And it would be nice to think the relationship is symbiotic—going both ways. Studies show that kids who grew up going camping have a deeper understanding of the natural world—and of becoming environmentalists and ensuring the protection of our wild places. Can you think of a more valuable experience than witnessing the interplay between the elements and living things?

But how do you camp without destroying fragile ecosystems? Here are a few things to keep in mind the next time you venture out beyond the traffic and malls:

1. Tread lightly. Watch your step and avoid trampling seedlings, wildflowers, and wildlife (that includes things that slither, hop, or crawl).

2. Leave the place better than you found it by picking up other people's trash along with your own. And keep your volume down so as not to disrupt the animals.

3. Pitch your tents and build your fires in areas that have already been used for that purpose. If you're desperate to commune with unspoiled earth, leave your camp where it is and meditate in that pristine locale instead.

4. Use only biodegradable products, and be careful to avoid the use of soaps—even the green phosphate-free

kind—in streams, creeks, and lakes. Why? Because while you're a temporary visitor, lots of fish and other animals make this their permanent residence.

5. Bring your own organic food for your adventure: Just figure out what you want to eat, pack it in reusable containers, and you're good to go!

6. Pack rags or microfiber cloths to use instead of paper towels. You don't want to be sitting among all of those majestic trees while rolling through roles of paper towels made from trees, do you? Now that you're wearing your green contact lenses, some old habits can look really out of place, can't they?

7. Always throw water on your campfire when you're done to prevent the fire from spreading. Droughts in many parts of the country have made conditions more dangerous than perhaps you're used to.

8. Stay on designated trails, and from time to time look behind you (as Tosh does in his bamboo garden) to make sure you're moving forward without leaving a trace.

9. Ironically, the camping manufacturing industry often uses toxic substances, just like any other industry. Before your first trek consider purchasing eco-friendly camping products and gear.

10. Look into being a volunteer for forest cleanup days in the national parks. If you're going to be in California, try logging on to www.totalescape.com.

11. For help finding the ideal hiking trail, visit www.trails.com for a comprehensive list of trails and topographical maps for hiking, mountain biking, paddling, skiing, hot springs, and climbing.

CHEWING GUM

Ever throw gum out your car window? Does swallowed gum really take *seven* years to break down and leave your system? Naw. Turns out, gum's digested and eliminated pretty much like food, and usually as quickly—unless you're a bird or a rodent. They can choke on your leftovers. Gum is also an environmental irritant. When it melts in the sun, it can end up on car tires and lead to the use of chemical solvents to remove it. In short, unlike an apple core it's not really biodegradable, so it's best left *inside* your car.

Camping Squared

Sometimes the idea of hanging out includes prolonged action beyond just an afternoon or weekend trip. Ever think about taking a chunk of your summer and going on an extended outdoor stay? If you've ever walked through a national park or wilderness area, you might have wondered who makes all those trails. Well, if you sign up with the Alaska Department of Fish and Game, you can spend a month blazing a trail in Alaska—and not everyone can say they've done that! A friend of ours went, and he said it was "awesome." He paid his airfare, he joined up with a super-fun group of kids, and they took a month to create a quarter-mile trail through the wilderness. And then they went hiking for a few days as a group. Hard work? Yes. Fun work? Yes! What a cool way to be of service and get community service credit for high school too.

If the idea of getting away for a month during your summer break to sleep under the stars, build trails, protect natural habitats, and become a champion for our national parks and forests with other teens (who may become lifelong friends) appeals to you, check out the nonprofit organization the Student Conservation Association (SCA) at www.thesca.org. Since 1957, fifty thousand teens like you in all fifty states have learned, grown, given back, kick-started their environmental careers, or just had experiences of a lifetime. This group is the largest of its kind, but it's not the only group.

go fish

"Give a man a fish, and you feed him for a day.
Teach a man to fish, and you feed him for a lifetime."
—CHINESE PROVERB

Fishing is one of those slow activities that harks back to the days when we lived in harmony with nature and knew how to feed ourselves—what a concept! There's nothing like sitting in a boat on a lake with your fishing pole draped over the side (as Linda did with her uncle as a girl), or standing by a stream and fishing from the glistening tumbled rocks of the shore (as Tosh did with his sixth-grade hiking class) surrounded by a cathedral of wood giants, waiting patiently for your first bite. As the sun streams through the pine needles and the wind carries their scent, you feel more connected and safe and peaceful than perhaps *ever*.

Your rod bends, you reel in the fish and clean it up, and the next thing you know you're enjoying this bountiful gift that came straight from the source. Thank you, refrigerator truck and PVC vinyl shrink-wrap, but your services will not be needed to make this healthy dinner happen. Amazing how that works.

You might be surprised that we're even talking about fishing in a green book, and the truth is, we don't have the heart to see fish squirm on our lines anymore. But fishing is still wildly popular, and people are going to eat fish and eat meat, no matter what. It seems better to us to do it naturally and in harmony than to think of fish as something that comes from a store or restaurant already done. These fish are often caught in massive trolling nets that destroy whole stocks at an astonishing pace. When Linda was a kid, having fish—or a roast or steak, for that matter—was a big deal, usually saved for a special Sunday night family dinner. The idea of eating animal flesh three times a day (as is now common) or even every day was unheard of in her home. You might want to start thinking about your level of consumption. *Is it something you could lessen?*

Fishing is becoming less accessible as urban sprawl eats up our wild spaces. Consider this chain of events: To satisfy the global need for wood and to make way for "growth," trees are cut down. The stream that ambled in the shadow of those trees heats up because the shade and much of the moisture the trees held and regularly released have vanished. The fish·can't spawn or survive in the water's hotter temperatures. Therefore, cutting down trees equals the loss of fish. And this isn't taking into account other fish-frying factors such as acid rain, drought, wildfires, mud slides, mining waste, pollution, and global warming. Yikes. Are you shaking in your wader boots yet?

If you're going to take up fishing, do your research to find a safe, uncontaminated area to fish from, an area without skyrocketing levels of mercury. You'll gain a deeper understanding of the natural order of ecosystems, your place within these systems, and how to care for them respectfully.

And if you're feeling adventurous, there are plenty of green recreational activities in the great outdoors!

being green outdoors

Sailing

If sailing on the big blue ocean floats your boat, you'll love knowing that it's one of the oldest means of emission-free travel. Choose a sailboat (or yacht) that's powered up and propelled by water or wind instead of fossil fuels. Or, if your parents insist on using an engine-powered yacht, suggest selecting one with an eco-friendly generator that puts the boat on autopilot, which helps cut back on fuel consumption and pollution.

Biking and Roller-Skating

Are there sidewalks or bike paths overlooking your favorite beach? If you're one of the one in eight Americans who lives in California, you can head to the beach and rent bikes, beach cruisers (no-frills bikes with low handles and wide tires—especially comfortable for riding on sidewalks and boardwalks), or roller skates for a day of exercise, sun, and fun. What could be more green than biking or skating? And since it's so much fun, you may decide to use your bike or skates more often. Did you know that if you rode your bike thirty miles a week instead of using a car (if you have one), you'd prevent fifteen hundred pounds of CO_2 from polluting the air?

Just moving your body outside makes it a green activity, as long as you're not using too many fossil fuels to do it. Some of the most popular green outdoor activities include:

- Green hiking—Get out and breathe the fresh air among rocks and wildflowers.

- Surfing—Check out the eco-friendly biofoam surfboards at www.sdsurfeco.com, actually stronger and lighter than most other boards. And there's even new surf gear like bamboo towels, organic surf wax, and sunscreen made from natural products such as green tea.

- Kayaking—It was good enough for the Native Americans, why not you? These days you don't have to cut down a tree to make your own kayak!

- **River rafting**—By using the power of the rushing water, you don't need a drop of petroleum for this activity. Not for the faint of heart, though. In other words, perfect for you!

- **Snowboarding**—This is crazy fun and green on a naturally good snow day because your speed comes from gravity—a renewable resource. Be smart, though. Those knees have got to last you.

- **Cross-country skiing**—This sport takes a lot of physical work, but there are stunning landscapes. And what could be greener than using your own lung and leg power to glide you through the trees?

In a race to improve its air quality in time to host the 2008 Olympic games, the government of Beijing spent thirteen billion dollars to clean up the city. China's environmental problems have become a source of great motivation for the country's youth.

go green exotic

Now that you're in a nature-protecting mind-set, what about carrying it with you everywhere you go? Travel is the one place—especially when you're staying in hotels and flying on planes—where it's easy to veer from your good eco-habits and become a little reckless—or downright wasteful. Starting with the endless supply of free drinks on the plane (coming from aluminum cans or plastic bottles), those little sample bottles of shampoo and lotion in the hotel, and the steady stream of free towels and maid service, life starts feeling like one big never-ending banquet table, with you as the very deserving prince or princess. Yeah, you've worked hard all school year, but can you wind down and relax without falling totally off the eco-wagon?

Greening Your Hotel Room

Many hotel chains now have green initiatives that give you the option of reusing sheets and towels, thereby greatly lessening your water and energy consumption. If you find yourself staying in a hotel that hasn't yet jumped onto the green bandwagon, you can help them get with the program by downloading a Green Hotel Initiative Guest Request Card at www.ceres.org. Hand it to the desk clerk when you check in. It lets the hotel know that you don't need your sheets and towels changed every day or your shampoo replaced if the bottle is still half full. And when you check out, there's a space on the card where you can give the hotel feedback about how environmentally friendly they've been.

Family Vacations

The next time your family decides to take a trip, see if you can suggest or help organize an eco-trip instead. You can go to Costa Rica, the Galápagos, or countless other places across the globe on green tours that minimize impact and support local sustainable cultures. Ecotourism was the 2006 buzzword of the year, according to the *New York Times.* Combining travel that preserves the environment while promoting the welfare of local people is a worthy trend.

According to the International Ecotourism Society, the market for conservation-oriented tourism is growing quickly; in 2004, worldwide ecotourism and nature tourism grew three times faster than the tourism industry as a whole. With upward of eight hundred million people traveling each year, that's a substantial percentage that can help boost economies rich in natural resources. While people flocking to pristine locales have the potential to harm anything and everything in their path, if this kind of travel is done under the proper conditions, the potential to provide incentives for conservation is worth the effort.

See if a beloved environmental nonprofit close to your heart leads outings that could bring you and your family to places you might otherwise miss. By joining up for an excursion like this you get to work on environmental projects with people literally on the front lines of change—and learn life-changing skills while doing your part. Much like the Peace Corps volunteers, eco-travelers work on projects in developing countries where they can see an immediate result to their efforts—perhaps building community buildings or setting up water pumps for grateful, thirsty villagers. Maybe you'll end up helping a scientist research something really cutting edge in a remote location you'd normally never have access to? Travelers are required to give a donation, so there's no free trip (free lunch, maybe), but the experiences are priceless. For a list of ecotourism resources, go to www.nature.org/ecotourism.

The Rainforest Alliance has an online guide, the Eco-Index Sustainable Tourism (http://eco-indextourism.org), where you'll find information on ecotourism in Latin America and the Caribbean. But we're not just talking about traveling to faraway places; you can do this close to home, too—which, remember, lessens your carbon footprint. For example, the Wisconsin Department of Tourism has a Travel Green Wisconsin program that encourages hotels and tour operators to be more environmentally friendly to protect the state's natural tourist destinations. Green is "in," so these things are popping up everywhere. See what's happening closer to your crib.

Air Travel

You can't think about traveling very far without seriously considering flying in an airplane. The problem is that air travel is one of the largest contributors to greenhouse gas emissions. The David Suzuki Foundation crunched the numbers and discovered that aviation accounts for 4 to 9 percent of the total climate change impact of human activity. And these emissions are produced at cruising altitudes high in the atmosphere, worsening the impact. With more than seven thousand takeoffs and landings per hour in this country, flying has become something of a normal everyday occurrence—much like taking the train used to be for commuters in the first half of the twentieth century. To do your part, see about taking that train instead. And fly direct whenever possible. Check with your carrier to see if you're able to purchase carbon offsets when you buy your ticket (most carriers offer this service), which will negate some of the carbon released into the atmosphere during your travels.

hanging out at the movie theater

Back at home, what's more fun than meeting your friends at the theater for a different kind of trip—taking your mind to a foreign or futuristic place or a fantasyland on the screen? Tosh and his friends love scary flicks. Maybe you do too? Think about it: Together you experience suspense, fear, relief, and jittery nerves as you jump out of your seat, scream, laugh, pretend not to hide your eyes, and then relive it with humor when it's all over.

But what's really scary is that 1.4 billion movie tickets are printed each year—and guess what happens to most of them? Uh-huh. They're trashed. The next time you buy movie tickets (or play, concert, or plane tickets), go online so you can print them at home on recycled paper. Back in that dark theater, when you're tempted to throw your stubs onto the floor with the overflow of your buttery popcorn, consider sticking your stub into your pocket to recycle it later. You're already doing this with your soda cans, right? Same thing, only easier!

CHAPTER SIX

GREEN WHEELS

Getting to where you need to go is a major green issue. Of course, walking or biking anywhere won't increase the size of your carbon footprint on the planet. But foot or pedal power aren't always options if you've got to get somewhere quickly or travel long distances. The second you step into any kind of motorized vehicle, you've got to start thinking about the size of that carbon tire tread! How can you make the greenest choices from among all your options? It's a real balancing act.

go mass to save gas

It's easy to make the greenest choice if you live in an area where public transportation—trains, buses, subways, monorails—is an option. You don't need a calculator to figure out that taking mass transit is the most eco-friendly way to get around if you're going to ride. Driving a car "costs" the environment about a pound of carbon dioxide per mile. If you drive ten miles to school each way, you're putting about thirty-six hundred pounds of carbon dioxide into the atmosphere every year. By contrast, in 2005 people reduced CO_2 emissions by 6.9 million metric tons—and saved three hundred forty million gallons of gas—simply by taking public transportation instead of cars. Taking mass transit also kept four hundred thousand metric tons of car-spewing greenhouse gases out of the air.

Cities all over America are making buses, trains, and subways even more eco-friendly by using alternative fuels and engines, using energy-saving brakes, lowering idling time, and improving routes. The more of us who take advantage of these mass transit options, the more eco-friendly the options will become and the more the systems will expand so everyone can use them. Also, since more people are choosing to ride mass transit for environmental reasons, you're joining an earth-friendly community every time you hop on board. It's definitely worthwhile to do the little extra planning it takes to put more mass transit into your life.

So it's a no-brainer to step onto the subway or bus instead of grabbing a cab if you've got those options in a major city. However, a lot of kids live where mass transit doesn't run as frequently or isn't as accessible. Even so, there's one form of mass transit you almost certainly have where you live: the school bus. The more kids who ride it, the more fuel-efficient it becomes; your school bus uses up just about the same amount of fuel whether it carries one passenger or forty. It's unquestionably the greener choice. Taking the bus is also the safer option; 55 percent of school travel-related deaths and 51 percent of injuries are caused by teens driving other teens. It's hard to miss these yellow behemoths all over town, but a lot of kids aren't riding them. Why not?

Because most kids would rather drive! An AP Statistics class at Analy High School in Sebastopol, California, did a study of how many teens drove to school, and they were blown away by what they discovered. Forty percent of students who lived within a mile of the school drove there every day—alone! The class found that parents and students were driving forty-two thousnd miles a week to campus, using twenty-five hundred gallons of gas, and contributing a whopping fifty thousand pounds of greenhouse gases to the atmosphere. Sadly, not even 20 percent of the students walked to school, and fewer than 5 percent biked.

Analy High School is probably pretty typical for a suburban high school, where kids have greener options but don't choose them. According to the Centers for Disease Control, forty years ago half of all kids walked to school; today just 10 percent do. Almost a third of the cars clogging the roads in the morning are taking kids to school, driving right by the school buses. So you have a real opportunity to change these statistics by taking the bus or other mass transit, and maybe inspire others and get them to challenge the idea that they "need" to drive to school. If you must drive, can you at least carpool?

CARPOOL VANISHING ACT

Only about 18 percent of vehicles on the road during rush hour use the carpool lanes. In Los Angeles more than half a million cars go through the popular intersection of the 405 and the 101 freeways every day! Next time you're on the highway, look around you and imagine that the car in front of you, behind you, and to the left have vanished. Pfft! Just disappeared. That's what the road would look like if every car carried four passengers instead of just one. Just think how much faster everyone would whiz along if three-quarters of half a million cars vanished.

Maybe what stops kids from using greener options to get around is the idea that it feels like too much of a sacrifice. Sure, taking mass transit or carpooling means surrendering a bit of independence and convenience, but how can you reframe that so it's not about *depriving* yourself but about *giving* yourself a different kind of experience? For example, carpooling is a great chance to hang with your peeps, relax, or finish last-minute homework. If you're going on a long trip, you can take turns driving and sharing costs. The more passengers in the car, the more energy you save.

And if you decide to leave the car in the driveway and bike, walk, scooter, or Rollerblade to school instead—maybe not every day, but once or twice a week—you won't get stuck in the gnarly pickup/drop-off line at school, with all the fumes and delays and grouchy crossing guards. And you'll save a ton of money on gas—an idling car can burn half a gallon of gas in a half hour! Plus you'll get to wake yourself up before class with some fresh air or exercise, or enjoy some private thinking time, or maybe grab an opportunity to look around and really notice what's cool in your neighborhood. Going car-free doesn't have to mean drudgery.

There are two more ways to reduce your carbon tire tread: share or rent! Wouldn't it be great to be able to use your own car whenever you wanted but hand over the headache of paying for gas, maintenance, insurance, parking, and washing to someone else? That's what you get when you "carshare"—buy a share in an organization that owns a fleet of cars, instead of renting or owning your own car. With carsharing, you pay a membership fee or pay for each use, reserve the car in advance for when you need it (by phone or on the Web), stroll up to the reserved parking space, and take your wheels for a spin. And you don't need to troll for parking spaces when you're done; you just bring the car to the nearest reserved space. It's a great option if you don't do a lot of driving, live in a city, and have access to the service. Carsharing is great for the environment, too: Researchers estimate that using one shared car saves the amount of energy that would be used by six individually owned cars.

There's also a small but growing business of car and limo rental companies whose fleets run on biodiesel, grease, electricity, or some combination. Some of the major rental companies offer hybrids. Right now prices are a little higher than for standard rentals, but the extra cost is worth it to know you're doing your part to help the earth.

pedal power to the people:
better biking

Chances are you did a lot more biking when you were little.
Didn't you love it then? Talk about freedom! Remember the
buzz of churning your pedals to blast up a hill, or feeling
your hair streaming behind you on the downhill? Now that
you're thinking of how to spend less time in cars, it's a great
time to put more biking back into your life. Try recapturing
all the great feelings you used to have when you were
pedaling away—and revel in not having to weigh the costs
of all those driving options.

The advantages are obvious: no greenhouse gases, and
your foot power's the ultimate renewable resource. You can
get a pretty good new (or used—think recycle!) bike cheap,
and then the only things you need are a good helmet, some
blinking lights, and a reflective vest if you bike at night—oh,
and a decent bike lock and a backpack.

Put bikes into the equation every time you think of going
out—running errands, going to school, hanging out with
friends. You'll be in the best shape of your life and feel good
knowing you're helping Mama Earth get there too. If you live in
a small space or don't have much storage, consider a folding
bicycle with a carrying case. They come in a variety of models,
set up in seconds, and ride like any other model. It's even more
fun to bike when you get all your friends on board. A growing
number of towns are starting programs to get people out of
cars and onto bikes. Investigate the bike paths in your area,
and if there aren't enough, consider meeting with local
officials about creating them.

school assembly on wheels:
AN INTERVIEW WITH SAM WEINER

Sam Weiner, a senior at White Plains High School in White Plains, New York, remembers the day he dreamt up Ride Your Bike to School Day. "I'd see so many individual kids driving just themselves to school. My friends and I counted more than five hundred forty cars parked on a campus of twenty-two hundred students." Sam thought that was a huge waste of gas.

He proposed Ride Your Bike to School Day to the principal, but the school couldn't sponsor it for insurance reasons. So he went to the police department, but they couldn't officially monitor the event unless Sam could guarantee a certain number of riders. So Sam decided to organize the event himself with the help of the Students for a Democratic Society club.

The first Ride Your Bike to School Day was a success, with more than fifty riders participating. Sam led the main group to the school, blowing a bugle back at every car that honked at the group. Students liked it so much that they've decided to make it a monthly event, weather permitting.

"There's always a lot of cheering," Sam says. "It brings a lot of different kinds of kids together." After each event they announce the winners, like the student who biked more than twenty miles to join the ride, one who pedaled his bike while lugging a huge electric bass guitar on his back, and one who rode all the way to school on a tricycle with a flat tire!

Sam's had his license for more than a year, and he gets the thrill of being behind the wheel. His advice? "Take a break from your car for just one day, and trust me, you'll have a good time. I honestly have more fun riding my bike than driving to school—and I make better time!" Sam hopes that Ride Your Bike to School Day will remain a tradition—he's already planning to donate his bugle to next year's seniors!

Bicycles Built for Two, Three, Four . . .

Bike-sharing, like carsharing, is a growing phenomenon, and another way to reduce and recycle. Here's how it works: Donated or purchased bikes are painted a uniform color—yellow and white are the most popular colors, but some folks go crazy with pink, green, you name it—so people know which bikes are part of the program. You either go to a single central location to borrow the bike or you pick it up at one station and when you're done drop it off at the station closest to your destination. It works on an honor system, with people paying either a coin deposit (refundable when you drop the bike off) or a small fee ahead of time to offset the cost of vandalism or theft. These programs got their start in Europe—there are more than sixty-two so far, in cities such as Paris, Brussels, Sydney, Stockholm, Vienna, and Barcelona—and are now starting to take hold in the United States. To get you started learning everything you want to know about starting a community biking program, recycling bikes, encouraging schools and business to get involved, and more, check out www.ibike.org.

Doing the Electric Slide

There's another option if you've got a lot of ground to cover but don't want to use a gas-eating moped or motorbike: the hybrid electric bike. Let's say you're traveling about ten miles but you don't want to get all sweaty pumping up hills or battling wind; an electric bike is a decent middle ground because it uses a lot less energy than a gasoline-powered car. You can buy one for between four hundred and fifteen hundred dollars. If you're a gizmo geek, there are even build-it-yourself kits. If you want a really stylin' ride, you can buy a conversion kit to turn a recumbent into an electric bike. Electric bikes are already huge in China, with more than forty million on the road, and sales in the United States are heating up too. Celebrities like Daryl Hannah look beautiful on their hybrid electric bikes.

making the car-carbon connection

If you don't live in a mass-transit-friendly area, driving may be more of a necessity, especially when longer distances and time crunches make biking a challenge. (There's no school bus where Tosh and Linda live, for example.) And if you're like a lot of teens, no one has to exactly twist your arm to make you jump into the car. We get it. You've waited your whole life to get your license, and now you just want to drive—but you know it burns up a lot of fossil fuel, and that's a serious drag.

Tosh has really brought the car issue to a head in our household. He's a teenage boy, so what would he mostly care about? Now that he's got his driver's license, dang, he wants to use it! How often do you think he has daydreamed about having a fast car—and a big, heavy, beefy one at that—the kind that guzzles gasoline as fast as he likes to down a can of soda? Plenty! He's tried a thousand different ways to justify buying one of those tricked-out babies with the money he's been saving since he was twelve from his acting residuals, and he has driven Linda crazy with his schemes. But at the end of the day, of course he could never do it—those gas guzzlers wreak havoc on the earth. (Depending on which source you believe, we currently import between seven and thirteen million barrels of oil per day!) So Tosh judges people who do drive them and is envious of them all at the same time. Maybe you can relate? No biggie. Now all we have to do is come up with between $80,000 and $100,000 for his new obsessions—the Tesla or Fisker electric cars he's currently salivating over!

So if you're going to drive, what are the most eco-friendly options? In the old days you had a few major choices to make: Standard or automatic? (Standard's harder to learn but uses less gas and gives you more control.) Gas or diesel? (Diesel fuel's more expensive, but diesel cars generally get better mileage and can be converted to run on grease—as you'll see.) New or used? (Used cars may not be as thrilling, but they're a lot cheaper.)

Automobile emissions are one of the biggest contributors to global warming—after all, there are an estimated 850 million vehicles on the roads throughout the world.

Fortunately, today you've got a lot more options that will get you thinking about how to hit the highway while minimizing harm to the environment. There are cars that use gas—a nonrenewable resource—more efficiently and cars that don't use gas at all. Researchers are coming up with some amazing alternatives to fossil fuels. Let's check out some of the most exciting developments.

Hybrid Cars

You've seen all the commercials and ads. No question about it. Hybrids have definitely hit the mainstream. The days of yearlong waiting lists are over, and just about every major manufacturer has sleek new models coming out of the pipeline. Experts predict there will be about a million hybrids hitting the road in the next few years.

The days of celebrities proudly barreling up to the hottest party in a gas-guzzling Hummer or Escalade are becoming a thing of the past. Today eco-conscious stars like Leonardo DiCaprio, Cameron Diaz, Maggie Gyllenhaal, Christina Aguilera, Johnny Depp, Luke Wilson, and Mick Jagger are pulling up to the Oscars and rock concerts in hybrids, so you know they're the new symbol of cool.

What exactly does "hybrid" mean? Hybrid cars run off two different fuel sources: gasoline and electricity. They basically switch back and forth between the two (the car's computer decides, so you don't have to) so that when you're stuck in traffic, you don't burn as much gas. This means that hybrids produce fewer emissions (because the car runs off a battery a lot). Most get upward of forty miles per gallon (mpg). The battery that powers the electric motor recharges while you're driving, so you don't ever need to plug it in.

In stop-and-start traffic (the kind you get more often in the city instead of on the highway) a hybrid is about 10 to 15 percent more fuel-efficient than a regular car. This means that if everyone in the country switched to hybrid cars, we could reduce our gas consumption by at least 10 percent.

Zap! Electric Cars

The electric car was actually invented *before* the gas-powered car—in the 1830s! However, gas- and diesel-powered cars were easier to operate and easier to produce, which is why we have the 150 million to 250 million vehicles that are on the road today, while as of 2005 there were only about sixty thousand EVs (electric vehicles) on the road.

In the 1990s, car manufacturers developed a generation of EVs that solved a lot of the problems of earlier models. So why didn't *these* stay on the road? A recent documentary called *Who Killed the Electric Car?* suggests that part of the reason was that the car manufacturers, the government, and gas and oil companies deliberately sabotaged efforts to make electric cars a widespread success because they didn't like the idea of consumers clamoring for cars that cost only two to four cents a mile to run—a fraction of the cost of gas.

The good news is that car companies are about to launch a whole new generation of more affordable EVs with longer-lasting batteries, a longer driving range, and a shorter recharging time—some even have solar panels on their roofs! Will Ferrell drives an electric car that costs "roughly thirty cents a gallon." Tom Hanks brags that he can get up to seventy-five miles per hour in his. All that and no emissions!

To be really green, look into buying a used electric car (you can sometimes find them for as little as a few thousand dollars) and powering it with a solar panel in your yard. Tosh found a new Mustang that was tricked out to run electric—also for the low, low price of $100,000. (No, he can't buy it. But a guy can dream, right?) But the aforementioned Tesla Motors and Fisker Automotive are the ones currently giving James Bond's Aston Martin a run for the money. They are still Tosh's faves! While the number of EVs is not yet close to that of hybrids, watch for a lot more of these cars to hit highway soon.

MAGIC ON WHEELS!

There's an electric car in development that's beyond exciting: the V2G, or vehicle-to-grid car. This car not only runs on electricity, but also *creates* it as you drive. When you're done running your errands, you plug it into a base station and sell the excess electricity to the local utility company. A consortium including professors and students from the University of Delaware are working on a prototype car that can go one hundred fifty miles without a charge. One million V2G cars on the road could actually generate the same electricity as twenty power plants!

Hydrogen Fuel Cell Cars

Imagine a car whose tailpipe emits water vapor instead of stinky gas fumes. That's the promise of hydrogen-powered cars, whose energy source is a hydrogen fuel cell. Right now there are only a few hundred of these on the road, and demand is limited, since the Department of Energy says there are only fifteen hydrogen fueling stations in the United States, ten of which are in California. That hasn't deterred *Entourage* star Jeremy Piven (Tosh's favorite actor on his favorite show), the latest celebrity to drive a BMW Hydrogen 7. Some scientists say that fuel cell cars are a good decade away from mainstream car sales. However, hydrogen is a renewable resource with a lot of promise, and researchers are trying to find ways to make these cars more energy-efficient, so stay tuned for more developments relating to this alternative fuel.

A Car That Runs on Air?

The Air Car sounds like something Tosh's science fiction teacher would dream up, but it's the real deal, running on nothing but compressed air while emitting even cooler air. It's the brainchild of a French Formula One engineer in partnership with India's largest car manufacturer and will go on sale in India and Europe in 2008. Labeled a "tailpipe dream" in *Time* magazine, this automobile can go up to seventy miles per hour and up to one hundred twenty miles per fill-up. It achieves its incredible fuel efficiency—try three dollars per fill-up instead of fifty dollars!—because it's so lightweight and because the compressed air produced by electricity is so cheap. Safety regulations threaten to keep the Air Car away from American markets for some time, but this is the kind of exciting innovation that makes our green eyes twinkle, especially when thinking about countries such as India, which may soon need to rely on exports to fill its growing energy needs. A car that runs on air would be a huge economic boon.

Which Is Greener: a Gas-Powered Car or a Hybrid Car?

So which car is the best for planet Earth? For most people the big question boils down to choosing between the two most widely available options: a gas-powered car (new or used) or a hybrid. We wish we could give you a one-size-fits-all answer, but like all the best things in life, it's complicated. Maybe you were thinking about a hybrid—or at least encouraging your folks to buy one—because a more fuel-efficient car is better for the earth. Or perhaps you had the horrifying experience of having to pay with your own money to fill up the gas tank—and suddenly your wallet is skinny enough to make it to *America's Next Top Model.* With gas prices soaring, you want to go with a car that gets more miles to the gallon.

The problem is that some of the hybrids don't live up to the mega-mpg hype. Linda has had two hybrids. The first was a small SUV—the car she used when she could no longer stomach the honking-big carbon tire tread of her beautiful luxury car. She ended up selling the hybrid SUV after only a year, though, because it didn't get even thirty mpg. The second, which she still has, is a hybrid car that gets nearly fifty mpg. She's much happier with this car, but she's still looking to find more efficient ways to get around.

So calculating your mpg and cost per mile are the most important things you can do to figure out how fuel efficient your car really is. Here's how to do the math:

Step 1: Wait until your gas tank is nearly empty (leave just enough so that you don't run out of gas), and then fill it up all the way. Write down the odometer (mileage) reading and the price of a gallon of gas. (And be sure not to top off your tank when you fill up—that spillage ends up in the oceans!)

Step 2: The next time your tank is nearly empty again, refill it and write down the new odometer reading and the number of gallons used.

Step 3: Subtract the first odometer reading from the second odometer reading; that's the number of miles you traveled between fill-ups.

Step 4: Divide the miles you traveled by the number of gallons you used; that's the miles per gallon (mpg) for that period.

Step 5: Divide the price per gallon of gas by the mpg; that's how much it cost for gas per mile to drive your car for that period.

Your mpg will vary from trip to trip. It'll be higher when you drive longer distances on the highway, lower when you're stuck in stop-and-start traffic. Calculate your mpg a few times to get an average.

Of course, you'll also want to compare how much it costs to buy your car in the first place. As hybrids become more popular, prices are falling. Also, depending on your state laws, if you buy a hybrid, you or your parents might even get some tax money back. All of this can make it cheaper to buy a hybrid than a regular new car. (For a great website to help you figure out costs and compare cars, check out www.fueleconomy.gov/feg/drive.shtml.)

When you buy a used car, you'll pay less than for a new car, and you're doing the kind of recycling we talked about in Chapter One. By reusing a car, you're keeping the roads clear of yet another vehicle and saving all the costs of making the new car and disposing of the old one.

That's the route we went with Tosh. For his seventeenth birthday, he got a used Honda Civic that we had had for years and that gets good mileage. Okay, it wasn't the sexy chromed-out vehicle of his dreams, but he was still excited because the wheels on the car still drove him to freedom. (Isn't that the point, anyway?) He no longer had to ask for a ride from his parents to get to auditions in downtown Los Angeles (although in the first few months he did have to deal with getting lost nearly every trip!). He could feel good about his eco-friendly choice. (And his parents could feel good about saving money.)

Of course, you could get the best of both worlds by buying a used hybrid car. With consumers demanding more of these, that market will only get hotter every year.

Obviously, when you're trying to decide which car does more for the environment, cost and fuel efficiency aren't the only considerations. Purchasing a hybrid isn't only about dollars and cents. It's also about doing your part to minimize impact on the environment by reducing your emissions and dependence on petroleum. Here's another opportunity to rethink. What do you want your choices to communicate about what you value? Horses under the hood, or impact on the earth? We smile every time we see another hybrid on the road. It tells us that more people are thinking about reducing their carbon tire tread. And again, if you choose not to drive or to take only mass transit, you're sending an even more powerful message: that you can get around without jumping into a car.

alternative fuels: putting a different tiger in your tank

Thanks to some amazing research advances, we've got a lot more choices not only in the kind of vehicle we choose to drive, but also in the kinds of fuel that make them run. Let's take a look at some of the coolest choices.

Biodiesel

Is it time for your car to eat its vegetables? Regular diesel cars run on diesel made from petroleum products. Biodiesel, however, is made from vegetable oil (soybeans, rapeseed, mustard, flax, and hemp are common sources), treated in a special way (no, you can't just dump a gallon of canola oil into your tank), and then blended together with regular diesel. Some manufacturers make biodiesel from chicken fat or fish oil; researchers are even trying to figure out how to convert algae into biodiesel.

There's a reason people are flocking to biodiesel. (Two hundred fifty million gallons were manufactured in 2006, up from seventy-five million gallons just one year earlier.) Biodiesel is nontoxic, renewable, and biodegradable. It reduces soot by 48 percent, hydrocarbon emissions by about 67 percent, and net emissions of carbon dioxide by about 78 percent. Another bonus: Using it instead of regular diesel also reduces certain cancer-causing agents in the atmosphere. Plus you don't usually need to modify your car engine to use it. It's also generally less expensive than regular diesel. However, critics argue that the corn and grain require heavy pesticide use and that biodiesel is not a viable long-term solution because higher pertroleum prices will lure food from the poor and hungry people of the world in order to provide alternative fuel to the world's wealthier drivers. Let's hope that's not the case. Switchgrass, which needs to be planted only once (it reseeds itself) and grows in many places where food crops can't thrive, may be one of the most promising biodiesel options yet. To find out more about biodiesel, including the manufacturer nearest you, check out www.biodiesel.org.

Grease

Maybe fast-food fries aren't the best thing for your body, but who can resist them now and then? But did you ever think about what happens to all the grease in the deep fryers once those fries have been flipped and sold? A lot of it ends up in—you guessed it—landfills. But now you can put that grease right into your tank! There's a growing market for WVO—waste vegetable oil—in so-called grease cars. Thousands of owners have snapped up diesel cars and spent anywhere from a few hundred to fifteen hundred dollars to convert the engines so they'll run on grease. (Most people do a dual conversion so cars run on both diesel and WVO, since oil freezes solid in cold weather and can clog the engine.)

Like using biodiesel, using grease cuts back on emissions, and grease is a renewable and nontoxic fuel. It makes the most sense to drive a grease car if you spend more time on the highway; hanging out in stop-and-start traffic means your engine will run more in the diesel mode, which eats up the savings (to your wallet and the environment) of running on grease. Right now grease cars are awaiting official certification by the Environmental Protection Agency.

Grease cars run on any kind of vegetable oil: new (which is called straight vegetable oil, or SVO) or used. You can usually get all the used vegetable oil you want— for free. Restaurants usually have to pay someone to take away their used oil—up to one hundred gallons a week—so they're happy to have a grease car owner take it off their hands for nothing. Of course, you can't just pipe the oil right into your tank; you have to filter it at home first, using a pre-filtration kit that separates the fuel from water, food particles, and other gunk your engine doesn't want. Owners say that filtering usually takes just a few hours a week. Since a typical diesel gets forty mpg, a fifteen-gallon tank will let you go about six hundred miles before the next fill-up. And while you're driving, don't be surprised if you get a little hungry; your car will smell something like doughnuts while you're cruising along. Maybe those fries aren't such a bad idea after all, *especially when the potatoes are grown organically*!

Ethanol

Did you know that Henry Ford's first car ran on ethanol? Ethanol is a kind of alcohol made from corn, barley, or rice husks (which is why it's sometimes called grain alcohol) as well as from scraps left over from logging or making paper. What's great about ethanol is that it comes from a renewable resource, reduces hydrocarbon and benzene emissions, and produces less carbon dioxide. What's not as great is that right now we spend a lot of energy growing the crops for ethanol and then producing and shipping it all around the country because we don't have the same kind of setup to pump ethanol as we do for gas. There are only about 175 ethanol stations nationwide. (In contrast, half of the cars in Brazil can use ethanol as fuel, and all of their thirty thousand gas stations have at least one such pump.)

Some researchers claim that it actually takes more energy to produce ethanol than you save by using it. Other studies have shown the opposite. Environmentalists are worried that it'll stress the earth too much—requiring too many pesticides and using up precious water and land that could be used for other crops—to grow the corn or other feedstock necessary to meet the demand for ethanol fuel. However, countries such as Germany, Sweden, France, and Spain are using ethanol successfully, and Portland, Oregon, became the first American city to mandate that every gallon of gas sold within its city limits contain at least 10 percent ethanol. Scientists are looking at ways to produce ethanol from cellulose and other sources so that it's more energy efficient.

In sum, the jury's still deliberating about ethanol, but it looks like if we can figure out a way to make it more efficiently—perhaps by relying more on using waste from other processes—ethanol might be a good alternative fuel option.

> Jay Leno owns a 1909 Baker Electric car that still runs on its original battery and was designed by Thomas Edison in 1901. It can go one hundred ten miles on a single charge!

driving greener with the car you've got

Let's face it: Most of us don't have the luxury of simply rushing out and getting the most fuel-efficient car. We forgot to be born heir to the Hilton Hotel fortune, and it's all we can do to buy lunch off-campus, let alone a few hundred horsepower. We've pretty much got to make the most of what's already in the driveway. So besides carpooling, how can you drive in a way that harms the environment the least?

Pedal off the Metal

Speeding not only ups your chances of an accident (seventeen-year-olds have the worst driving record for accidents, which is why your parents go into a coma when they get your insurance bill) or a ticket, but it also burns up a lot of excess fuel. If you drive ten miles over the sixty-five-mile-an-hour speed limit, it can gobble up 10 percent more gas—and depending on your car, your tailpipe might spew even more emissions. How's that for an incentive to be a law-abiding citizen! (Keep up the good behavior and your insurance rates will fall too—a nice reward, huh?)

Keep Your Tires Tight

You know better than to let your tank go dry, but when's the last time you checked the pressure on your tires? Do you even know how? (It's actually really easy. You can buy a tire pressure gauge for a few bucks at an auto supply store or have the attendant show you how to use the one at the gas station.) Making sure your tires are properly inflated means you'll drive more safely and it'll also save you gas. Most car tires are underinflated, and taking yours to the gas station for a quick sip from the air hose can improve your mileage by 3.3 percent. Doesn't sound like a lot, but if you drive six thousand miles a year, underinflation "costs" you an extra $150 to $250 a year, or about seventy-two gallons of gas. And each gallon burned dumps about twenty pounds of carbon dioxide into the atmosphere.

Get the Junk out of Your Trunk

If you're carrying around a lot of extra weight, your engine has to use more fuel to lug everything around. People are worth the extra pounds; junk isn't. Do a check on the backseat and trunk and clear out stuff you're not using.

Trip Yourself Up

You burn up the most fuel starting your car. Before they head out the door, Linda and Tosh take a minute to figure out how they can combine a bunch of errands instead of making a separate trip for each little thing. And they figure out the most efficient route to each stop, which saves time, money, and energy.

Stop the Stop-and-Start

Ever speed up to a red light and then stomp on your brakes and sit there? That little maneuver—mashing on the accelerator and then jerking on the brakes—uses up to 33 percent more gas than skipping the whole hurry-up-and-wait deal. So aim for a smoother cruise. It'll save you big bucks and help keep the air cleaner. Plus, it's a lot less annoying to your passengers (not to mention the drivers watching you roar up toward them in their rearview mirrors).

driving it all home

Every day you step out into the world, which means that every day brings you a fresh choice. Hop into the car? Hop onto your bike? Step out in your trusty kicks? Sure, there are going to be times when you've just got to get behind the wheel, but the point here is that you don't want to drive an auto on autopilot. With some rethinking and reframing you can drive with a green light and a green conscience straight ahead.

CHAPTER
SEVEN

GREENER SCHOOLS AND CAREERS

N ow that you've been thinking about how to make your home greener, it's time to think about the other place you spend most of your time: school. (Did you think we were going to say the mall?) Most of what we've been talking about up until now is about what you can do as an individual to live a greener life. School gives you a terrific opportunity to take everything you've learned and work with others to make even bigger things happen. It's where you can work with committees to start environmental clubs and organize green events. It's where you can figure out how to work in teams with teachers, advisers, principals, school board members, and other people in the school community to make a difference. Even if all you do is show your classmates the eco-friendly school supplies that are out there, you can have a powerful green influence.

This chapter is also a chance for you to look ahead and see how you can make being green even more of a way of life. A lot of school is pretty abstract. People are always telling you that you should do well in school so you can get into a good college, so that then you can get a good job doing . . . what? Maybe college is years away, or perhaps it's something you just don't think a lot about; it's just part of a fuzzy future that may or may not interest you. We urge you to keep an open mind. Maybe allow yourself to daydream about the idea that, wow, there's this really cool place out there where there are no parents, you get to pick your own courses, and there are tons of other kids your age doing cool things.

We want to make the idea of a green future feel just a little more real to you. The truth is, there are a ton of amazing, exciting adventures you can have—jobs and internships during the summer, careers after you graduate—some of them in fields you probably don't yet know exist. How cool would it be to make big bucks doing something really meaningful—maybe even helping to save the world?

But right now let's start with what you can do to help friends, classmates, teachers, and educators make the school you're in more eco-friendly. It's a lot of fun getting more involved with green issues at your school, and you can probably get community service credit for volunteer work. When everyone else is padding their résumés in this competitive job and college market, won't it be great to be able to put your green efforts on yours with a clear, green conscience?

green school supplies

Whether you're groaning or champing at the bit come September, there's something undeniably cool about having new school stuff—you just feel like you're getting a fresh start.

Before you head off to the office superstore, though, make the most of the opportunity to rethink and refuse. Check out all the notebooks you ditched in June; could you recycle old notes and handouts and use up the leftover paper? Can you give your old pencils, charcoals, and other art supplies a fresh sharpen instead of buying new? If your backpack zipper's busted, would it make more sense to take it to the tailor or dry cleaner to get a new zipper put in for ten bucks, and then wash it to make it look new instead of springing for a new one? This means your old backpack can avoid that express ride to the landfill.

SMALL BUT SIGNIFICANT

Can something as small as a staple harm the environment? According to Friends of the Earth we could save up to one hundred twenty tons of steel a year in this country if ten million office workers (or students) used one fewer staple per day! Staple-free staplers are an amazing innovation—cutting a hole in the paper and threading flaps together on the underside. While not good for more than five sheets of paper (and the staplers are made of plastic and thus require valuable resources to manufacture), they're yet another example of green innovation taking place all around us.

Educate your school about eco-friendly school supplies: from sustainable pencils; hemp backpacks (with solar chargers); recycled paper, pens, and scissors for your art projects; staple-free staplers; and 100 percent recycled-content file folders, let's look at what you can invest in to go green at school.

Paper

Picture a tree that's a hundred feet high and sixteen inches wide. According to www.idealbite.com, that's how much paper the average American uses every year. How many kids are there in your school? That's a pretty sizable forest getting chewed up for trig and bio homework.

Bright white paper may look appealing for copies and notebooks, but it uses mercury and dioxins during the bleaching process. Instead choose recycled paper with a high percentage of postconsumer waste (PCW) content. Look for PCF—processed chlorine free—paper that's also PCW. The PCW label means the manufacturer is reusing materials left over during production—for example, paper trimmed while making newspapers or books, or aluminum cans too dented to be filled or the paper, aluminum, or glass you actually tossed into the recycle bin. Look for products with high percentages of postconsumer waste materials. You're putting less stress on the environment and encouraging manufacturers to make the most of the recycle chain.

You may have to do some digging to find PCW paper. Websites such as www.greenearthofficesupply.com are a good place to start. For a guide to brands, check out www.conservatree.org/public/localsources/copypaper.html. Or type "green paper supplies" or "green office supplies" into your search engine for local suppliers. At home, Linda and Tosh use paper notebooks made from composted and ground-up banana peels, coffee grounds, maps, and even old recycled money (Tosh's favorite). We've even heard of paper made from elephant dung!

Writing Implements and Art Supplies

Choose refillable pens and pencils. You can get pens and markers made from recycled materials, and pencils, too. (Tosh was initially embarrassed to use his during the four-hour SATs, but they ended up being stronger than the "normal" kind.) There's even a refillable pen made from cornstarch that will biodegrade within a year after you're done with it. And did you know that you can buy 100 percent biodegradable crayons made of soy for art projects? They glide easier without flaking and include brighter colors, too.

Notebooks and Binders

If you can't squeeze a bit more use from last year's supplies and you're on the hunt, again, look for products made with a higher percentage of PCW. At home we use binders made from recycled cardboard.

Backpacks

If it's time for a new one, can you give your old backpack to a local shelter or other needy organization? And while you're on the prowl for that new carryall, check out ones made from recycled materials (rubber, even pulverized old soda bottles!) or from organic hemp or cotton. You can even find solar backpacks or messenger bags that will not only carry your gear, but will also charge your cell phone, camera, or MP3 player on the go from photovoltaic panels stitched into the top of the bag. You can find battery packs that go along with your bag to store any excess energy your bag generates.

Electronics

A single sunny day will power a solar calculator through the toughest calc exam. Don't you wish your brain worked the same way? (Or maybe it does!) More and more companies are manufacturing computers while minimizing the use of toxic materials. Also look for those that have take-back programs in place that will let you turn in your old computer for recycling for free or for a modest fee (usually about ten bucks).

The Electronic Product Environmental Assessment Tool (EPEAT) can help you figure out which desktop and laptop computers are the most environmentally friendly; check out www.epeat.net. In just the first six months of sales of computers registered as green by EPEAT, the Green Electronics Council reported *major* energy savings. For example, they saved enough electricity to power 1.2 million homes for a year, prevented 56.5 million metric tons of air pollution, and kept 41,100 metric tons of hazardous waste out of landfills.

Lunch

If you're wanting to bring your lunch to school and are thinking about investing in a reusable lunch bag, there are lots of options. You can find cool, colorful bags that scrunch up nicely in your backpack, or rigid-sided ones, all made out of recyclable materials. We mentioned vintage metal lunch boxes in the Introduction. Right now there are more than eighteen hundred of them on eBay, so you can go retro with Strawberry Shortcake, Knight Rider, or Scooby-Doo.

If you've ever purchased prepackaged food, it probably came in plastic containers with fitted lids, and by now your pantry could be overflowing with them. These work great for lunches too. Wax paper or brown bags are more readily biodegradable, but you can also try using a rinsed out and dried resealable plastic bag to help you green up your day.

green from the first day

Although big chains and superstores are finally figuring out that consumers want green school supplies, it can take a little more effort to hunt them down. So here's a great idea for a community service project that can get your school thinking green and help raise money at the same time. Or perhaps you can get your school business club to set this up, or, if you're super-enterprising, do it on your own. Some schools or PTAs do fund-raisers by creating ready-made school supply kits. Families simply send a check to the PTA, and the kit is waiting for the student on the first day of school—no running around the aisles or feverishly searching the Web. Maybe you could contact your PTA or PTO or school board and offer to help them research an eco-friendly back-to-school supply kit. If enough families sign on, you might be able to negotiate cheaper rates. You'd be helping a lot of families get involved in being eco-savvy, and now that we think about it, where would your eco-initiative look impressive? . . . Uh-huh . . . *on that college or green career application*!

And speaking of fund-raising, if you're like Tosh, you're sick of having to sell the usual wrapping paper, T-shirts, and candy to family friends and neighbors. Why not organize fund-raisers with green products—there's even recycled wrapping paper, if you must. It's a terrific way to support the school and introduce classmates and their families to green options. And if you're doing a bake sale, why not use the opportunity to sell a few products from local growers who frequent your farmers' market. You know, your new BFFs!

getting your school on board

In Tosh's chemistry class, the paperwork was insane. "We cut down ten trees just for my homework," he jokes. How can we rethink this? Does your school have a recycling program? Tosh, Hannah Goldner, and their buddies in Valencia High's Environmental Protection Agency ordered and distributed dozens of recycling cans on their campus.

Are they purchasing textbooks made from maximum pre- and postconsumer recycled paper? Can you convince your teachers to go paperless more often and give out lesson plans, study packs, and homework online, and maybe even accept papers online?

If your school already thinks green, they may have LED or CFL bulbs in place—but how good are people about flicking off those lights when classrooms are empty? Are windows propped open during the winter so that precious heat—and kilowatts—rushes outside even as students roast inside? Can you organize an effort so that computers are turned off at regular intervals, and especially before long school breaks?

Do the teachers who cover consumer science, home economics, and related subjects include information about organic food, eating locally, and sustainable living?

The Advanced Placement course in Environmental Science (commonly known as APES) is one of the newest Advanced Placement courses offered. Right now it's available in about twenty-five hundred schools, with about fifty-two thousand students taking the AP exam. APES is a fantastic way to see if you want to consider studying the environment more formally in college. Does your high school offer this program? If not, could you request that they add it to the curriculum?

How about your school cafeteria? Does it have any organic or locavore offerings? Could you persuade them to grow some greens right on school grounds? Manhattan's Calhoun School, with their Eat Right Now lunch program (serving healthy and often locally grown food) and fourteen hundred square feet of green roof (complete with flowers and grass) proves that you don't need a lot of real estate to pull this off. Does your cafeteria use reusable trays, cutlery, plates, and glasses, or do they rely on disposables? Perhaps you're inspired to see what you can do to change that.

GREENER SCHOOLS, SMARTER KIDS

Want to convince the principal and school board to green up your school? Show them the results of the 2005 survey of green schools done by Turner Construction, a company dedicated to creating sustainable buildings. According to the survey, 70 percent of districts with green schools reported that students improved their performance on exams. The Global Green USA Green Schools Report noted that students who get more natural daylight in their classrooms—a major feature of green construction—progressed 20 percent faster in math and 26 percent faster in reading in one year than students who learned in environments with the least amount of natural light.

Does your school invite speakers to raise students' awareness of environmental issues at assemblies? Maybe you can use some of the money from your green fundraisers for this.

Consider checking out what other teens are already doing on your campus. Perhaps your school already has a club in place that can help you advocate for more sustainable practices—Advocates of the Earth, the local chapter of the Students for a Democratic Society, or others. When Tosh joined the environmental group at his high school, he was surprised to see that he was one of only two boys who showed up. An added bonus! If there aren't any clubs, consider starting your own so you'll have a lot of friends to help you lobby. You might want to request a meeting with a teacher, adviser, principal, superintendent, or school board to propose some ideas for helping kids become more involved with greening up your school. Whatever you do, try to do it diplomatically.

To find out other ways to help green your school, check out these websites: www.nrdc.org/greensquad and www.greenschools.net.

You could gain valuable speaking experience (and maybe even community service credit) for going to middle and elementary schools to share information on conserving energy and getting involved with green projects with younger kids. Teens can be powerful role models, as this next interview reveals. (And notice how this next green teen's passion led to a green major in college—a stepping stone to her green dream career. *Now say that three times fast!*)

grass girl:
AN INTERVIEW WITH KATE CONSROE

Kate Consroe of Potomac, Maryland, can't recall how old she was when she began caring about the Chesapeake Bay. Was it during that fourth-grade trip when she and her friends rode an oyster boat through the calm blue waters? Or in middle school during a three-day excursion crabbing, kayaking, and "marsh-mucking"—playing in marsh mud. Soon, Kate learned the Bay was in trouble. Waste and excess nutrients from farming and development were flowing into it at an alarming rate, smothering plants and oysters, clogging fish gills, and causing excessive algae growth that blocked light to underwater plants. The Bay had developed dead zones where nothing could live.

Kate had an idea. As a junior Girl Scout she had helped an older girl earn her Gold Award—the highest honor in Girl Scouting. Kate was now sixteen and old enough to go for the award herself. The challenge? To create a project you're passionate about that meets a need in your community. Kate was inspired by the Chesapeake Bay Foundation's Grasses for the Masses program that teaches kids how to grow grasses in their homes and classrooms to increase oxygen levels in the Bay, to hold sediment where it belongs, and to provide habitat for baby fish and crabs. It was the perfect model.

For her Gold Award she took her presentation to classrooms ranging from kindergarten to ninth grade, and when she was met with apathy, it didn't last long. "They'd go, 'Okay, whatever,' but then they'd get into it, asking questions. One little girl suggested we drain the Bay and add brand-new water! That's not the solution, but at least she was thinking about it," Kate said, laughing.

Kate showed several fifth-grade classes and eleven Girl Scout troops how to grow grasses in containers the size of kitty litter pans. In late spring they planted them in Clopper Lake, part of the Chesapeake Bay watershed. The project took nine months, but Kate knew she'd found a lifetime career path.

"I have very strong opinions about environmental issues," says Kate, now majoring in environmental science at Dickinson College in Carlisle, Pennsylvania. Her goal is to work in sustainable building design and environmental education. "If we can teach each new generation to be more environmentally aware, it's going to be easier to win the battle. Everything's connected—it's about lots of little pieces. There were so many problems with the Bay, and what I did was help with one little piece of the bigger picture."

green campuses

When it comes to colleges, campuses are getting greener than ever. When *Sierra* magazine did its first article on environmentally friendly colleges in its November/ December 2007 issue, e-mails poured in with students singing the praises of their alma maters.

Sierra Club chose Oberlin, Harvard, Warren Wilson College, the University of California system, Duke, Middlebury College, Berea College, Pennsylvania State University, Tufts, and Carnegie Mellon for its first Top Ten ranking, but chances are good that any number of colleges will be vying for the honor in upcoming years.

What's really changing among colleges and universities is that they're not just reworking courses to reflect the eco-friendly majors students want; they're rethinking how they build and rebuild their campuses and power them, as well as how they house and feed their students. Many college campuses are focusing on new green construction and practices. For example, the University of Vermont has committed to meeting or exceeding all LEED certification standards developed by the U.S. Green Building Council for all of its new construction. And UC Berkeley is the first American university with a certified organic dining facility, something the students were asking for!

Some colleges and universities have had green majors for a while; others are just getting on board. If you want to check out a prospective school, you'll need to plug more than just "environmental science" into your search engine. For example, Cornell's College of Agriculture and Life

Sciences is the hub of environmental study on the Ithaca, New York, campus. You can delve into anything from ecology to landscape architecture to food science to the science of earth systems. If you're interested in an earth-friendly major, search for these topics and more:

- Agricultural science

- Biology and biological sciences

- Business

- Ecology

- Engineering

- Environmental science

- Environmental studies

- Forestry and environment

- Natural resources and conservation

- Parks and recreation

- Plant science

- Science and technology

Some colleges and universities are not only offering eco-majors; they're really building their whole college philosophy around sustainable living. Founded in 2003, the Eco League is the only official consortium with member colleges dedicated to putting environmental awareness in the front and center of their curricula. Alaska Pacific University in Anchorage, Alaska; College of the

Atlantic in Bar Harbor, Maine; Green Mountain College in Poultney, Vermont; Northland College in Ashland, Wisconsin; and Prescott College in Prescott, Arizona, are all dedicated to "environmental liberal arts." To learn more, check out www.ecoleague.org. Students on these campuses don't just study the environment in the classroom; they live in eco-friendly dorms (many cleaned with only green products), lobby for sustainable products to be sold in campus stores, and spend a lot of time working closely with local communities on green projects.

If you want to do more investigation into the kind of college that might be right for you, obviously your guidance counselor is a major resource. Check out the Sierra Club article at www.sierraclub.org/sierra/200711/coolschools. Also look at the guide to the top fifty environmental colleges from *Kiwi* magazine; you just register for free online and they'll let you download their issue at www.kiwimagonline .com/green-college-report. For some great tips on what kind of environmental school would suit you best, check out www. environmentalschools.org. If you type your intended major into the College Board College Matchmaker (at www.collegeboard.com), you can learn all about the ins and outs of what you're interested in (including the requirements you'll need to apply) and narrow the search by any number of parameters: geographic location, size of the student body, tuition costs, and the like.

If you're really curious, it's easy to take a 360-degree virtual tour of most colleges online. You can look around in the comfort of your own room—and no need to offset the carbon footprint of a campus visit! If the day comes when you want to get more serious about choosing a college, there's nothing like visiting one to get a feel for how deep the school's commitment goes to being eco-friendly. Check out the cafeterias, dorms, and student unions. Are they walking their talk? Check out the flyers for clubs, speakers, and other activities on campus—is green a priority? Do the dorms compete to see who can use the least amount of energy? (Check to see if there are any flyers for Turn Out the Lights or Meet Me in the Dark contests.) Do they have arboreta, swamplands, rivers and lakes, hothouses, or other living laboratories close by for exploration? What about semesters abroad to get an international perspective on sustainable living? Visit the career center. How involved is the school in helping its students find green internships during summers and green jobs after graduation?

California is for many reasons, including energy efficiency (which is double that of Texas) and investments in green technology, the greenest state in the nation. More Californians recycle than vote! (More than 50 percent.)

summertime, and the living is green

Want to see if a green career is a good fit? What better way than to dip your toe in with a summer internship? Spend a few weeks working for a nonprofit (we'll talk about them below), travel abroad to get an international perspective, or stay on campus and work with a professor whose work inspires you. If you want more information on internships offered by the Environmental Protection Agency (along with great advice on careers and scholarships), check out www.epa.gov/highschool/careers.htm. The Environmental Careers Organization can even help you find a paid internship: www.eco.org.

green careers, green paychecks

The green world is expanding so rapidly; why not jump aboard and put your energy and passion for the environment into a lifelong career? The Bureau of Labor Statistics predicts that the career market for environmental scientists will grow more rapidly than the average career market through at least 2012. This is partly because we're finally waking up to how desperately Earth needs our help. It's also because as governments around the world put more rigorous guidelines in place to make manufacturers create more eco-friendly products, we'll need a lot more scientists helping make wishful thinking into concrete reality.

Don't think that a green career means you've got to be a scientist. Consider this: There's a green angle to just about any career! Here is just the tiniest fraction of the possibilities:

Love the Law?

Become an environmental attorney and represent environmental groups or help develop important new public policy. With all the new and impending legislation intended to help businesses become more energy-efficient, we're going to need a lot of lawyers to help turn guidelines into action plans and help companies and the government enforce them. Lawyers are on the front lines of some of the most exciting environmental causes. For example, the lawyers at the Natural Resources Defense Council (NRDC) have won major court cases that have protected a hundred million acres of land in Alaska and have protected the Arctic National Wildlife Refuge from oil drilling, and the lawyers have proposed legislation to put the polar bear on the endangered species list. NRDC has also gotten more than two hundred companies to stop selling old-growth wood products, which will save untold millions of acres of rain forests. See what can be accomplished when like minds with a little schooling under their belt come together and spearhead a cause?

Ready to Trump Trump?

Get a business degree and use it to help eco-friendly companies rake in the big bucks. Or want to help turn Wall Street green? You can't open the newspaper or a news magazine and not see some incredible new financial or career opportunity emerging in the green world. This hot new field is called "clean-tech," and it's growing by leaps and bounds. In the first three months of 2006, people poured $34 million into investments in Silicon Valley alone. Six months later the investment was up to $290 million! By December 2007 the green venture capital investments— the money paid to get green companies up and running— were up by 45 percent!

Member of the Debate Team?

Become a spokesperson for a green issue. There are thousands of nonprofits focused on green causes. They're everywhere, but you'll find most of them in state capitals (because that makes it easier to work with state and local governments), Washington, D.C. (because the Capitol and the White House are just down the street), and New York City (because the UN is there and groups want to reach out to the international community). If you've got a passion, there's almost certainly a green nonprofit for it. Does your heart sing for birds? Maybe the Audubon Society is for you. Does inner tubing down a sparkling clean river give you reason to live? Sign up to work with Riverkeeper or the Waterkeeper Alliance. Do you love city parks? Join Bette Midler's New York Restoration Project (NYRP) and help the flowers grow. Want to help keep our national parks pristine? Check out the National Parks Foundation and the Sierra Club. The website www.guidestar.org lists more than nineteen thousand environmentally aware nonprofits, so you're sure to find one that speaks to what you love the most.

You can even work for a great cause in a sustainable environment! In September 2006 the Thoreau Center for Sustainability opened in New York City; it's one of the few office spaces there to meet LEED certification, and it houses the Tides Foundation, which does a lot of green grant work.

Love *Project Runway*?

Go into green textile design and work with sustainable fibers or fabrics that incorporate solar panels for PDAs,

MP3 players, and the like. This market isn't just for the Birkenstock crowd anymore; cool green clothes and textile designs are everywhere. More than thirty companies in North America have been certified by Oeko-Tex Standard 100, the international standard that guarantees that products are free of harmful substances. So you won't only be wearing a cozy fleece from Polartec that's been okayed by Oeko-Tex—soon you might be designing the next line!

Into Architecture?

The market's booming for green construction. The U.S. Green Building Council, which issues the LEED guidelines for environmentally friendly office buildings, is about to issue guidelines for homes, and people are clamoring to be part of the movement. More than ten thousand new homes are being built to the new standards, with cool features like that recycled blue-jean insulation we talked about in Chapter Three between the walls, computer-operated vents that pull in fresh air, and green roofs that grow actual food! Since the devastation of New Orleans by Hurricane Katrina, green architects have played a significant role in designing and planning new housing that is harmonious with the city's distinctive style and sustainable, with features like solar panels, wheatboard (instead of particle board), FSC-certified wood, and soy-based foam insulation. All over the country, owners are demanding architects and contractors who can renovate or retrofit their existing homes to lessen the environmental impact. Or maybe you'd like to be a community planner—figuring out how to lay out homes, offices, and shops with minimal carbon footprints and maximal sense of community spirit. Think of the satisfaction of greening up an entire community! According to *Plenty* magazine, Minneapolis has a park within six blocks of every residence, and forty-three miles of bike paths! Some very proud people designed that and made it happen, and maybe that's the type of job for you.

Want to Make Green with Your Green Thumb?

Get involved with organic gardening, start and run a food co-op, work with conventional farmers to help them convert to organic farming practices. You've probably noticed how much easier it is now to buy cage-free organic eggs and organic milk in your regular grocery store. That's because, as we talked about in Chapter Two, organic farming is going gangbusters. Licensed farms had sprung up in all fifty states as of 2005. And since organic crops can do up to 100 percent better during drought, the smart money's on this way of farming as we all become more concerned about rising temperatures.

Want to Be a Green Chef?

Go to a culinary school and train to become a raw foods or organic chef (or think about opening your own establishment or a specialty catering company). According to the National Restaurant Association, more than half of restaurants where people spend at least twenty-five dollars per meal offer organic choices on the menu.

Love to Walk on the Wild Side?

We talked about eco-travel in Chapter Five, and you know how quickly that market's growing. Maybe you'll be guiding folks through the rain forest on a zipline in Costa Rica, or educating them about tortoises on the Galápagos Islands, or helping break trail in Alaska. Or you might want to join organizations like the International Ecotourism Society, which promotes the well-being of local people as well as conservation of the environment. As ecotourism continues to grow, you can play a role in making sure it does so responsibly.

Love to Teach?

Get your teaching certificate and help raise the next Generation Green!

If you can dream it green, there's a career out there for you. The fields are changing by the minute. Follow your passion and you'll be heading in the right green direction. To learn more about eco-friendly careers, check out these websites:

- http://environmentalcareer.com
- http://jobs.treehugger.com
- http://opportunityknocks.org
- www.sierraclub.org/careers
- www.greenbiz.com/jobs/careerfaq.cfm
- www.enviroyellowpages.com/Resources/Jobs/index.html
- www.ecobusinesslinks.com/environmental_jobs.htm

STEP UP
AND SPEAK OUT

E very place you go, you have a chance to step up and get involved, to speak out, offer a suggestion, and make a difference. There's power in numbers. Individually and collectively, if you ask for change, you can create it. This chapter offers specific suggestions for what you might want to get involved in, what to say, and where to do it.

In case you're feeling at all intimidated, thinking that you're just one person who might not be able to do much, here are a few teen stories to help motivate you. You can find many of them and others like them at www.actionfornature.org. What they did wasn't necessarily glamorous, but these teens saw a need, got involved, and enriched their lives and futures in the process. See if any of these fellow Generation Green comrades make you think, *Hey, that sounds like something I might want to try!*

1. **Like father, like son.** Garrett Rappazzo, fifteen, of Castleton, New York, says he got the idea of organizing a massive tree planting campaign at his school from his father, who did the same thing forty years earlier. "For as long as I can remember," Garrett says, "my family and I have always planted trees together." Mobilizing fellow students and the local business community, Garrett recently planted fifty white pine seedlings at his school, assuring a greener future for his children, too.

2. **"Pump 'em up."** When nine-year-old Savannah Walters of Florida heard about how driving on underinflated tires in our country "squanders four million gallons of gas every day," she was determined to do something and adopted a catchy phrase, "Pump 'em Up." Now thirteen years old, Savannah goes door-to-door in her neighborhood with ninety-nine-cent tire gauges, showing adults how to get better fuel economy by putting the right amount of air in their tires. Savannah has also built a website (www.pumpemup. org), lobbied Washington, spread her campaign to ten states, and been featured on *NBC Nightly News with Brian Williams*.

3. **Don't drink the water.** Testing the water on nearly twelve airlines, Zachary Bjornson-Hooper, sixteen, of Alamo, California, made a troubling discovery: Some airline water is contaminated with unsafe levels of harmful bacteria. Zachary's findings were confirmed by the

Wall Street Journal and then by the U.S. Environmental Protection Agency, and drinking water on airlines is now inspected by the U.S. government. In 2005, Zachary was chosen by *Teen* magazine as one of twenty teens who will change the world.

4. Green bill. She's green, but not in political savvy. At fifteen, Stevia Morawski in Silver Spring, Maryland, worked with the Montgomery County Student Environmental Activists (MCSEA) to do the unthinkable: pass a bill in their county that required it to purchase 20 percent of its energy from wind power. Two years later, Stevia serves as the Public Relations Coordinator of MCSEA.

5. I'm a bird-watcher. She's not flighty. Gabriela McCall Delgado, sixteen, was selected as a 2006 International Young Eco-Hero for compiling a photographic booklet of more than sixty-five birds in Humacao, Puerto Rico, including endangered and threatened species. Using a slide show of her photos, Gabriela has given talks to professional, student, and community groups across the United States and Puerto Rico, raising awareness of the need to preserve natural bird habitats.

6. Open space. When ten-year-old Brian Meersma of West Windsor, New Jersey, saw more and more scenic land in his town being developed, he took action. He got involved with Friends of West Windsor Open Space and raised two thousand dollars by soliciting donations to help save additional land from development. Invited to Washington, D.C., Brian spread the open-space-preservation news to members of Congress.

7. Save the bear. Don't mess with Mollie Passacantando; she may be only an eight-year-old girl, but this native Virginian is an inspiration to green teens everywhere with her resolve to save an entire species. Mollie launched a popular pro-polar-bear blog and collected more than two hundred letters asking that the polar bear be placed on the endangered species list. Mollie was invited to speak to a large audience at Climate Crisis Action Day in Washington, D.C., and has been nominated with eleven others for an International Young Eco-Hero Award. Check out her blog at www.savethearctic.blogspot.com.

8. The long walk home. After getting lost during a walk in the woods near her home, sixteen-year-old Samantha Ellis of New York got serious about marking forest pathways. Enlisting friends and family, she marked trees along a five-mile stretch of popular hiking trail. Thanks to Samantha, now hundreds of nature lovers and hikers can confidently walk without fear of losing their way.

9. Nesting in New York. Fifteen-year-old James Quadrino of Staten Island, New York, realized something terrible happened to birds after a fire: They had no place to nest. James builds specialized birdhouses and places them during nesting season in areas where the native bird habitat has been damaged. For saving the lives of so many birds, James was honored by the president of the United States and awarded the Environmental Youth Award in the East Room of the White House in 2005.

10. Can by can. Thirteen-year-old Tayler McGillis of Toluca, Illinois, says he doesn't have much time for watching TV or playing video games. He has cooler things to do—like collecting more than twenty thousand pounds of aluminum cans. Tayler has walked more than one hundred fifty miles on local roads in his area picking up recyclable material. After donating more than ten thousand dollars to Habitat for Humanity (builders of homes for disadvantaged Americans) in 2007, Tayler was awarded the prestigious Environmental Youth Award in Washington, D.C.

We've found that a good way to get involved is to pay attention to what really interests you. That's how the teens mentioned above have been able to make a difference—because their green cause of choice wasn't forced upon them but fulfilled an inner desire to meet an outer need. So, begin by watching where your thoughts go throughout the day. Notice what catches your eye and holds your attention. If the idea of climbing trees sounds better than spending a day at an amusement park, something to do with trees might be the logical place for you to start.

> In one of India's poorest states, Patna, the capital of Bihar, a ten-acre farm has been converted into a bio-reserve by Abhishek Bharadwaj, fifteen, Achala Parmar, fourteen, and Wartika Pande, thirteen—three school children among many others who have been planting trees and greening a city where there's only approximately one tree for every two thousand people.

specific suggestions for stepping up and speaking out

To Your School Board

Be bold. Go to the next school board meeting and ask to share your ideas for a greener school with board members. (Most likely the adults present will be grateful to see you there taking a leadership role, so speak up with confidence!) Volunteer to be on any information-gathering team. Would you and your friends like to start a Ride Your Bike to School Day like Sam Weiner did in White Plains (see Chapter Six)? The next school board meeting (usually held once a month) might be the place to bring up your ideas to see about gaining support or even funds for things like more bike racks on school grounds, greener food in the cafeteria, fun green fund-raisers, planting a garden or additional trees on campus, establishing a green community outreach program, forming an environmental club for students, purchasing recycling bins to spread throughout campus, fixing water fountains to encourage kids to buy less bottled water—you name it!

Approach Your Local Community and Town Leaders

Sometimes you get more done by going to the top. If you're having trouble encouraging your school board to fund your idea, you might want to try venturing out into the community and meeting with leading businesspeople or town leaders (perhaps even the mayor!) to see what kind of support you can enlist. Perhaps even drop by the local paper to see about publicizing your endeavors. This strategy also applies to nonschool endeavors, like establishing an organic open-air green market, or a Really Really Free Market, or perhaps an eco-fair (with organic food, clothes, art, and home and beauty product vendors), or a concert in the park!

In the Grocery Store

Find the store manager and ask that the store stock more local and organic foods. If you find that the labels on cans and bottles are hard to follow (or are too vague), ask for clearer, more understandable labeling of signage in the food aisles. (You shouldn't have to be an honor student to figure out the difference between something labeled all-natural or organic or pesticide- and antibiotic-free.) If your store doesn't already offer inexpensive reusable bags, ask the store to carry them to encourage people not to use plastic bags or to use biodegradable plastic bags instead.

In Stores and Other Public Places

Why are so many stores, restaurants, and movie theaters so dang cold? Have you ever forgotten to bring a sweater to the movies and sat shivering the whole time? If the food in the coffee shop case will spoil if the place gets too warm, couldn't they just make the cases more chilled and energy efficient, and leave you, the customer, to sit in comfort? If you don't speak up, why would they change? The employees at one coffee shop, when asked, told Tosh they didn't mind the cold because they were moving around. But when his Internet was down for a week and he took his laptop inside to get some homework done in sunny California in the summertime, he had to bundle up in a ski parka because "sitting around" left his teeth chattering! Instead of copping an attitude, Tosh patiently explained the issue to employees and asked questions. He was given a form to fill out and send to the "home office" somewhere far away, which he never received an answer to. But he has noticed that every time he steps into that shop, the manager makes a point to say hello and walk over to the thermostat to lessen the chill. Make your needs known. Someone just might care about your experience after all!

At the Library

Ask your local library to sponsor more readings and lectures from authors of green books, and to carry a wider selection of environmental books in general. Tosh's grandmother was very involved in the Friends of the Library club in her hometown and attended organic gardening classes held on the grounds of the library, in conjunction with a meet-the-author signing of a gardening book and green home talks given by the author of a green design book. In this Internet age, we're losing our connection to librarians, who we used to depend on to know exactly where to find just the obscure piece of information we needed. Think about stopping by your library soon to make this face-to-face connection. You'll only enrich your experience of your community.

At Your Local Coffee Shop

If they don't already carry it, will they consider stocking fair-trade coffee? And if your local coffee shop carries cups and to-go carriers made of Styrofoam, tell them that's a no-no and to use more eco-friendly packaging with recycled content—especially paper products (cups, carriers, and napkins) that are made without chlorine bleaching, a process that puts potentially carcinogenic dioxins into the waste stream. It's okay to speak out and ask! The reason companies like McDonald's and Starbucks are using these greener paper products is because consumers have asked for and demanded the change.

IS YOUR COFFEE FAIR OR UNFAIR?

We consume a fifth of the coffee in the world here in the United States, but most of us don't know that many field-workers work in horrible conditions and are forced into slavelike cycles of poverty and never-ending debt. Fair-trade practices let you know that the coffee you're buying was grown and purchased under good and *fair* conditions. The certification is demanding, and prices are set to a minimum, ensuring credit to farmers and their communities, which positively empowers women and children as well.

At Local Restaurants

Ask to speak to the manager and request that the restaurant carry food made from local organic ingredients and, again, that they serve fair-trade coffee and organic beverages. If you're looking to do public service for school, ask if you can help arrange donating the restaurant's leftovers each evening to local food banks, and then use this as a platform with which to get other restaurants to do the same. What about hosting organic or raw-food cooking classes, bringing in coaches for positive publicity all around (for your group, the restaurant, and the coach). Maybe you'll get your lessons for free for your efforts? Restaurants are the ideal place to meet people and set up programs and host events for any group—whatever your cause. And there are so many to choose from. Ah, so many options, so little time!

Become a Joiner, Even If That's Not Your Thing

Maybe you don't trust "the system," as in politics. Green is beyond politics. It's beyond red, white, and blue. People who have been apathetic in government are often highly motivated in the green movement because the environment isn't discriminatory—it affects every one of us. Love of the natural world offers people on both sides of the aisle the opportunity to join together to work for the greater good, knowing that your efforts will protect both your mama and your future children. Whether it's a charity that works with politicians to affect change, or a particular political candidate you're hoping is worth your great green trust, getting involved is something to look into. Your planet needs you.

In December 1992 the big forest companies in Sweden committed to stop logging in mountain forests—the result of an international boycott. Money talks. Activism works. The mountain forests were saved because people demanded the forests' protection.

Write to Your Elected Representatives

Today it's easy to find websites for your local, state, and national representatives. Write to them and tell them what you're concerned about and the changes you'd like to see made. Tell them you're aware of the issues and their voting record, and let them know the many ways in which they can help secure the future of Generation Green.

GETTING THE WORD OUT!

Creating an e-newsletter will help galvanize support for your cause. You'll need to include a good photo so people feel a sense of connection to you and your message. Figure out what you want to say, and then find someone smart, other than you, to proof your finished text! Next, gather names and e-mail addresses. Send your passionate, positive, and powerful messages out every week or month around the same time, and keep them long enough that they add value to your readers' lives but not too long that they overwhelm.

Find Role Models

One of Linda's role models is younger than she is—but Linda still looks up to her! Julia Butterfly Hill was only in her early twenties when she reignited passion in the environmental movement in the late nineties. You've probably heard of her—she's the media darling who climbed one hundred eighty feet into a thousand-year-old redwood tree named Luna and wouldn't budge despite hovering helicopters; blinding rain, wind, and snow; and near constant harassment from the timber company who owned the land—who did just about everything except shoot her down. Julia's goal? To save an old-growth stand of trees slated for the big saws. Did it work? You bet—and it made her into a worldwide hero.

When Julia first climbed into Luna, she thought she'd be there for three weeks, tops. She ended up living in those branches for 738 days without touching the ground. She climbed into Luna because she wanted to help the forests. She didn't know what an activist was or how to be one, but she had grown up climbing trees and knew she could do that. . . .

sitting **pretty**:
AN INTERVIEW WITH JULIA BUTTERFLY HILL

Julia's obviously very courageous, but what does someone do who's never spoken out before, or maybe thinks they're too young to make a difference? "Who you are is exactly who you're meant to be," she says. "You are enough! Everywhere we look we see messages that we're not enough, that we don't *have* enough. We're told we need the new car, new clothes, the right 'look' that changes every season. But each and every one of us is more powerful than we can possibly imagine. When I first began my tree-sit, I was belittled and made fun of because I was young and female. But the longer I stayed there, the more being a young female became an asset because I was doing something that no one had ever done—not even the oldest or strongest of men.

"You need to trust your intuition and be open to guidance—even when others might make fun of you or attack you, and even when you're questioning yourself. I call these moments the 'choiceless choice,' when we hear that inner voice and could choose to silently walk away but a force greater than our fear compels us to speak up and take a stand."

Julia's parents say she was always stubborn. "If I felt strongly, I'd say or do what I wanted even if it got me into trouble. I was adventurous and wanted to experience life at my own pace instead of the more conservative pace of my parents. The great difference now is that I have learned how to direct my stubbornness into good causes.

"That doesn't mean I wasn't afraid. It's okay to be afraid. But take a deep breath and know that once you make a commitment and step into it with courage and humbleness, you'll do and be more than you could imagine.

All 'extraordinary' is, is 'extra ordinary.' Extraordinary people are completely human and recognize their own ordinariness but don't let that stop them from doing wonderful things."

In Julia's case, the power of "One" made a huge difference, and she believes the same is true for you. "Every single choice we make impacts our world because no choice is made in a vacuum. The question we ask ourselves is not, 'Can I make a difference?' Because everything we do and say and even think makes a difference. Rather, the true question is, 'What kind of a difference do I want to make?' Our lives become examples that inspire others to join us even as we look for creative ways to reach out, connect, and grow. The individual does make a difference, and the more we connect with one another, the more we grow the One that we all are."

Julia's latest book, *One Makes the Difference*, includes a detailed chapter on speaking up by using the media and becoming an activist/protestor (which she did masterfully).

be light green!

Being green or socially conscious doesn't have to be serious. In fact, it's more fun when it's not. So think about it: With your buds and BFFs you can do something fun—even silly—to create awareness for whatever issue you're passionate about. Do you and your friends like to hike, dance, read, plant trees? What's your passion? Saving the rain forest? Organic farming? Addressing global warming? Helping endangered species? There are organizations for every green idea under the hot sun. Get involved—either by yourself or with your friends—or both. Giving feels good. And if you do it with your posse, it can be all the more fun. Here's an idea . . .

Adopt-a-Highway

Ever watch *Seinfeld* reruns? Tosh has been obsessed with *Seinfeld* episodes for forever! One of his faves is the pothole episode, where Kramer adopts a freeway mile and thinks he owns it—that it's his to do whatever he wants with. So he removes those "annoying little bumps on the lane lines," telling Jerry, "Well, I had to pull 'em up if I'm gonna widen the lanes!" Hilarious! Most states have an Adopt-a-Highway program, where you adopt a piece of public road, and it becomes your responsibility to keep it clean. You might not want to try to bring the more-legroom-concept of a first-class plane flight to your stretch of highway mile like Kramer did, but you'd probably enjoy the good-deed feeling of removing trash, not to mention seeing your name on the highway sign.

Unbelievably, people still throw beer and soda cans, bottles, wrappers, and cigarettes out of car windows. Shame on them! They leave an ugly mess to clean up, but not on *your* road. Get out there and clean up your street, literally.

This green practice is so popular in Missouri, in fact, that more than one hundred thousand volunteers have picked up thousands of bags of litter, mowed hundreds of roadside miles, and planted countless flowers, trees, and shrubs. Currently there are 3,772 groups in the program that have adopted 5,281 highway miles. In some states, like North Carolina, prison inmates pick up millions of tons of trash from the highways each year—because people enjoying their freedom feel the need to toss fast-food wrappers and soda cans out the window as they speed down the road. Go figure.

To find out how to adopt a stretch of highway in your area, do an Internet search or contact your local county maintenance office. Ask to speak to an Adopt-a-Highway coordinator who can assist you on the terms of the program and then help you select your or your group's stretch of road to adopt.

leaving a green legacy

Linda received a wonderful e-mail recently from Marty Kollar, a woman who has lived in Europe for the past twenty-five years and can hardly believe how wasteful Americans are in comparison. After reading one of Linda's magazine articles on recycling for Delta's *Sky* magazine's Green Scene department, she concluded her letter to

Linda with this thought—which seems to us the perfect way to close this chapter, by reflecting on how our unique contributions collectively add up:

"The Egyptians will be remembered for the pyramids and we will be remembered for our mounds of garbage."

Wow. Something to think about.

How do you want to be remembered? What action could you take today to step up, speak out, and start crafting a greener life for yourself and our world?

A DAY IN A
GREEN LIFE

Is your head exploding yet? That's a good sign—means you're still with us. You could probably use a few more visuals with all of the suggestions we've given you, so this chapter's all about putting together everything we've talked about. Sound good? We'll start by walking you through a normal day, first as a "typical" teen would do it, and then we'll show a rewind with greener choices instead—using our green, greener, and greenest headings to give you creative options. (We heart choices!) Try making up your own. Some of ours will seem cheesy or silly or too idealistic—for us, too—but they're meant to get you thinking in your own green style. No matter how you choose to green up your day, let these examples reinforce the idea that all of your days are filled with hundreds of big and small chances to be green, and they all count!

waking up

Typical

Your alarm next to your bed blares. You hit the snooze button a few times and then make your way to the bathroom, ignoring the need to rush as you lumber into the hot steam-filled shower. Ten, twenty, thirty, forty, fifty gallons and twenty minutes later, Dad knocks to warn that you're late. You slather on soap or body wash, then shampoo, stopping to glance at the ingredients—what are some of these names? The list reminds you of chemistry class. You've heard that some beauty products can be toxic, but hey, the smells are off the hook. You rinse off a few more minutes—man that hot water is addictive! You get out, dry off with a synthetic towel, and throw it onto the floor. You brush your teeth with the latest fresh-breath-whitening-formula paste and let the water run while you check yourself out in the mirror from all angles. *Hmmm . . . Would the Katie Holmes new glam-chic haircut look dope or dorky on me?* You massage your face and body with lotion you bought at the pharmacy that promises an acne-free dewy complexion, a future without wrinkles, and a sun-kissed glow without the sun—a miracle in a jar. You roll on a sweat-and-odor-stomping deodorant and an intoxicating perfume—a fragrance you bought at the mall for cheap, cheap but that smells like you paid the big bucks.

Green

Your alarm across the room blares. You shut it off and then head into the bathroom. You take a five-minute shower and brush your teeth at the same time as you rinse your hair, careful not to get shampoo into your mouth! Your new organic soap and shampoo smell fresh and rinse clean. You get out, dry off with an organic cotton towel, and hang it back up to dry. On your body you rub in lavender-scented paraben-free lotion from Whole Foods or Wild Oats, and on your face you use Trader Joe's oil-free face version. You apply talc-free mineral face powder and toxin-free mascara and lip gloss—all of which you've researched on the Campaign for Safe Cosmetics website at www.safecosmetics.org to. (Just because you're a green teen doesn't mean you can't still be a lip-gloss-aholic like Linda! You just have to know the safe brands to choose from.) It's going to be a hot day, so you use your aluminum-chlorohydrate-free deodorant.

Greener

Your alarm across the room goes off. You get out of bed, turn it off, stretch, and make your way into the bathroom, where you determine that you're pretty clean from yesterday's five-minute shower, so today will just be a quick rinse-off instead. That takes all of about one minute. You dry off with a 100 percent organic cotton or bamboo towel and hang it back up to dry. You pull out the health-food-store brand toothpaste and see if you can brush with fewer than four swigs of water from the cup sitting on the sink. . . . Yup. Easy breezy. You forgo your old fragrance (the one you recently found out contains phthalates—linked to cancer) and dab on a vanilla-scented essential oil instead. You're smelling mighty sweet! Your eco-friendly lotions, makeup, and deodorant, and a quick brush through your hair, leave you looking prom-ready. *Okay, that's a stretch.* But at least ready for first period.

Greenest

Your cell phone alarm across the room chimes. You get out of bed, turn it off, and make sure your solar charger is unplugged for the day. You head to the bathroom, where you determine that you're all good from yesterday's five-minute shower, so today'll just be a quick sponge bath and face splash before getting ready. At only three swigs of water while brushing your teeth, you've beaten yesterday's water usage; you smile knowing you just hit your personal best. You've been living and eating clean so your complexion looks fab and you don't sense the need for deodorant. The only thing left to do is dab on a little eco-lotion and vitamin E lip balm to keep your kisser . . . well, kissable. Oh, and you throw your hair up in a fun, flirty ponytail. Now you're good to go, gorgeous!

getting dressed

Typical

You try on one of those three pairs of great jeans you just got at the "mall crawl" last week. You're still buzzing inside when you think about how your favorite store had that huge sale and you got a ton of cool pairs of jeans for half off! Love it when that happens. You throw on one of the supercool tops you bought on eBay that got shipped across the country from a great vendor you've learned to trust—that's a relief because the price was so good that you were hoping you wouldn't be disappointed or have to ship it all the way back! You finish off your very hip look with the latest pair of cool boots out of your many pairs— gotta keep it fresh, so you have a lot to choose from.

Green

You put on the organic jeans you bought at a boutique in town, and one of your organic sweatshirts, too. It bothers you for a second that the companies who manufactured them aren't local, but you cut yourself some slack, knowing that supporting organic farmers, free-trade practices, and mom-and-pop stores are a step in the right direction. You throw on your cowboy boots, which are gorg. No one can even tell they're made of vinyl—aka leather free. The coolest thing is that you look great without sacrificing on comfort or your growing green resolve.

Greener

Today you're sporting the hot new vintage jeans you picked up at the thrift shop last month. You paid, like, five dollars for these ones, but they're a designer brand and were once expensive, so you scored. You throw on a T-shirt you bought at the same place—made from organic cotton with a globe, smack front and center. You strut in front of the mirror, liking the fact that you're making an Earth-loving statement today. Your kicks are some newfangled hemp material you found at the co-op, and they actually feel really good on your feet. Nice surprise!

Greenest

You throw on a cute top you got at a clothing swap from a friend, and the eco-hemp pants you found at the thrift. You can see dark clouds forming out your window, so you grab that cozy organic cotton hand-loomed thick sweater you bought at the farmers' market recently and tie it around your waist. It's so soft you'd think it was flannel pj's! To top off your ensemble, you slip into last year's sneakers. . . . Why? Because they're still feeling fine and comfy. Nuff said.

leaving your room

Typical

You pack up your cell phone and leave the charger plugged into the wall. You grab your backpack as you head out of your room, your stereo blaring. Your desktop computer is humming, but it always makes weird noises anyway, so, oh well. You stop to try to remember if you turned off the overhead heat lamp in the bathroom, but never mind. . . . There's no time. Hopefully Mom will check before she heads out for work like she usually does.

Green

You pick up your cell phone, unplug the charger from the wall, and take your laptop with you, loving that it uses up to 80 percent less energy than your old desktop. You head out of your room, turning off the light and making sure your stereo is off too. You can't remember if you unplugged your electric razor, so you walk to the bathroom to double-check. Yes, you had even put it back into the drawer!

Greener

You take your cell phone from your dresser and put it into your backpack. No need to unplug the charger. You did that last night after a quick charge before you fell out. You pick up your hemp backpack as you head out of your room, turn off the LED light, and flip off the switch to the power strip that goes to your printer and stereo. Electric razor? You never even bothered buying one; you knew you'd hardly ever use it, so why waste resources? But you do a double take to make sure your sister's hair dryer is unplugged and *not* vampire sipping valuable electricity all day—that would be so three years ago!

Greenest

The cell phone you use only for emergencies (yeah, we know the odds of this, but humor us) is still charged from last week and turned off. The solar charger hasn't been plugged in for days either. You pick up your funky hemp backpack as you head out of your room, turn off the LED light, and flip the switch on the power strip that goes to your printer and stereo. Hair dryer? Negative. You and your sis are air-dry teens all the way today. You check the family laptop on your way out, and it too is off for the day.

grabbing breakfast

Typical

You drive to the Golden Arches, idle the car for ten minutes in the drive-through, grab a McD's breakfast and a hot coffee in a throw-away cup. You stop at the deli to buy bottled water for the scorching temps forecasted for later today. Then you drive to school, gassing it because you're especially late.

Green

You have a quick breakfast—maybe a homemade power bar (see www.generationgreenthebook.com for an awesome recipe for these), organic cereal with organic milk, or organic cage-free eggs and sprouted wheat toast. You grab an old plastic bottle, refill it with filtered tap water, and put it into your backpack to have with you for the day. You put a few dollars into your wallet to spend at lunch on a fast-food veggie burrito. You've got plenty of time this a.m., so you swing by the local library and drop off your dad's latest home improvement book on your way to school so he doesn't have to make a separate trip.

Greener

You have that same quick breakfast and throw the waste into the countertop composter. You fill your eco-bottle with filtered water and grab the organic lunch you packed last night in your reusable lunch sack. You catch the school bus and talk with your buds about an eco-surf-camp you'd like to try for a week this summer, and about where you're all going to meet this weekend before the big game.

Greenest

After eating breakfast, doing your countertop composting, filling your eco-bottle with filtered water, and packing up your organic lunch, you and a few friends ride your bikes to school. You arrive at your first class clearheaded and rosy-cheeked—ready to brave even the most boring lecture. "What are you so happy about this morning?" asks the usually grumpy gal who sits next to you. "What's in your breakfast cereal?" You eyeball the doughnut in her hand and wonder where you'd even start. You're quite sure your natural endorphins are the result of your healthy breakfast and exercise—so worth it, anyway—but you laugh it off and change the subject. Maybe if she asks again tomorrow.

lunchtime

Typical

At lunch you drive off-campus with friends for pizza and Supersize sodas. You throw all that packaging into the trash bin on your way out of the restaurant and stop by the local mini-mart on your way back to school so you can grab a candy bar and some gum to give you energy at the end of the school day. Big lunches like this often leave you sleepy, but they're so tasty that they're worth it, right?

Green

You alternate eating on campus a few days a week and going out for veggie burgers, bean burritos, or veggie deli sandwiches on the other days. You ask for minimal packaging (no thanks on those extra napkins, hot sauce, utensils, condiments you know you aren't going to use) and on the days you forget to bring your own drink container, you take recyclables home with you to be recycled or reused. You've packed an organic chocolate bar (that donates proceeds to an endangered-wildlife charity) with you in case your energy starts fading later this afternoon.

Greener

If you live near school, you walk home for a healthy homemade meal or tasty leftovers. Sometimes you bring a few friends with you or go to their houses, resisting the urge to raid their refrigerators by making sure you've stocked up beforehand on great snacks like organic popcorn, salsa, and organic blue corn chips. Maybe you include a few healthy vegetarian dips like guacamole or hummus from the deli or health food store. You're increasingly energized by the fresh food and fresh air you've been inhaling. Liking what it feels like to look and feel great, you're determined to keep it up.

Greenest

You hang out with your friends in the quad or courtyard while eating the vegan tofu bologna and soy cheese sandwich on whole wheat you made last night. You pass around slices from a few apples off your tree—the flavor's amazing! You take your reusable lunch sack back home with you to be used again tomorrow. Your green-light approach to eco-living is starting to rub off. . . . Even Al Gore would give you a standing O! You notice that each week more and more kids are bringing their lunches to this area. Could it be that you're starting a trend? Being green really is cool.

after school

Typical

Finally, the school day's over! You drive home and race through your chores so you can go out tonight. You run a load of laundry, using whatever soap was cheapest, then mow the lawn with the power mower. Dad wants you to water the plants with that brand of plant food he bought at the garden center, so you make sure to wear gloves because you don't want to get any of it on your hands. (You did once and it stung.) After chores you cruise over to the gym to work out. Then you head out to the mall to find a diversion from the homework already weighing down your weekend plans. Ugh.

Green

You carpool with some friends home from school. Then you get your ab and arms workout in by mowing the lawn with a hand mower. You plant a few new heads of lettuce in your organic garden and scatter organic coffee grounds and organic mulch under the plants and trees—something you do about every six weeks. Then you ride your bike to the gym to work out with your buddies, meet at the mall to see if the latest organic line of clothes has yet to hit the big chains, and then drop by your friend's house to get a jump on your studies.

Greener

You take the bus home from school before working out with the hand mower in the yard. You water the plants with rainwater from the water butt (the barrel or clean garbage can by the side of your house at the end of your rain gutter). Dad used compost on the plants, so you don't need to use any fertilizers. You and your friends decided it was a "no shop" day for anything besides food, so you skip the mall—too tempting—and meet up with your group of buds to play basketball at the Y.

Greenest

You walk or ride your bike home from school. No need to mow the lawn or water outside because the native landscaping you did earlier this year is thriving. The drip system connected to your gray-water tank is connected to a surprisingly easy and affordable satellite weather system that has it all covered when rain and dew aren't enough. You ride your bike to the open-air market, pick up some cool stuff for a picnic, and put it all in your carryall. You and your friends meet at the library to work on a project for school that's not due for eight weeks but that you want to get a head start on. (Okay, Linda's clearly dreaming . . . but this *could* happen, couldn't it?)

it's friday night

Typical

It's Friday night! You drive to get fried chicken with your friends for dinner, and then it's off to a night of paintball, where you ruin a good shirt with blue paint. Bummer. Afterward you roll to a late-night diner for a burger and a shake. Then it's off to a friend's house for video games before driving back home.

Green

You take the bus to Olive Garden for vegetarian soup, salad, and warm bread before meeting up for a movie with a bunch of your buds (remembering to keep your ticket stubs to recycle at home!). You avoid buying snacks that use a lot of packaging, and focus on the plot of the movie instead of your habitual sweet cravings. You ask the man behind the concession counter if he could please pass on your request of healthier snacks to his bosses, and he hands you a special request card, which you fill out in thirty seconds. That was easy.

Greener

You invite kids over to movie night at your house and suggest that everyone ride their bikes or skateboards over for veggie chili and garlic bread beforehand. The weather's right, so a few friends decide to sleep over outside under the pitch-black sky, and you compete to see who can spot the first shooting star of the night.

Greenest

You bike to the park, where you meet your friends for a picnic before you all chill out listening to a local band that plays some really good tunes. You find the perfect spot for some stargazing, good conversation, rockin' MP3 music (powered by rechargeable batteries, of course), and hanging out. Then it's back home to finish that great article about eco-travel you found the other day.

after dinner

Typical

It's your job to clean up after dinner, even though you were out with your friends. Mom wants you to "spit shine" (ew, how gross does that sound?) the kitchen. You spray down the counters with whatever stuff she bought on sale. You don't mean to be a spoilsport, but it's been a long week and you don't feel like rinsing out tonight's soup cans and pasta sauce jar, so screw it, you throw all the recyclables into the regular garbage. No big deal. It's a drag to hand-wash the dishes, so you throw 'em all into the dishwasher and run it even though it's only about a third full. At least the counters are neat now and it looks like you got a lot done.

Green

You clean the counters with Begley's Best green cleanser or vinegar and water. You wash the dishes by hand using water sparingly, or, if the dishwasher is full, you run it and then leave it open before the dry cycle kicks in so the dishes can air-dry. Or you push the air-dry button and leave it closed overnight. Before going upstairs to check your messages, you run the washing machine, using green detergent to help safeguard the oceans as well as your family. You don't remember why you convinced your mom to buy the phosphate-free laundry soap . . . something about detergent sitting at the bottom of the ocean for years. In your quest to stay informed, you'll Google it!

Greener

You put the dishes into the dishwasher and inform Mom why you won't be running it yet—because it's only half empty. She's cool with that, impressed that you've thought this through and aren't just blowing off the chore. You commit to the few seconds it takes to rinse out the recyclables, knowing you'll feel good tossing the dry cans and jar into the right bin in the a.m. You sweep up the dog hair, coffee grounds, and toast droppings that seem to be everywhere (dang, your dogs, little brother, and dad are messy!) and toss it all into the countertop composter. It's nearly full, so you walk it out into the yard and mix it into the large outdoor composter.

Greenest

You clean the dishes with the least possible water usage. You feed the indoor plants with the salad-and-veggie-washing water. You recycle everything and use only water or healthy cleaning products on the dirty surfaces. You visit the composter and stand in awe as you see how quickly your family scraps have turned to lush, dark earth (crazy, but true). Maybe tomorrow you'll mix the new earth in under the fruit trees? You're on a roll with living green lately, so if it's a nice day, you promise yourself to hang your clothes on the outdoor line instead of using the dryer. The clothes smell so fresh that way!

at night

Typical

You run a bath, wash your face with acne products from the drugstore, and then toss the towelettes into the trash. You wonder for a second about what kinds of chemicals you're washing down the drain, but if they were really that bad, they wouldn't allow them in the stores, right? You brush your teeth with the water running, and then hop into bed between poly/cotton sheets.

Green

You skip the bath and use a washcloth, which saves thirty gallons of water. You're psyched you bought that nontoxic mascara, mineral makeup, and face lotion at the health food store recently because when it all washes down the drain at the end of the day, you know it's safe for everyone and everything it comes in contact with. You brush your teeth with the water off, and then hop into bed between organic cotton sheets.

Greener

You skip the bath and use your washcloth and nontoxic face wash to cleanse your mug. You brush your teeth with the water off, and then hop into bed between organic cotton sheets. Now you check around your room to make sure you've unplugged everything you can so no electricity's wasted while you sleep.

Greenest

You skip the bath and brush your teeth. You slay the energy vampires, make sure the heat's turned off, and slide into bed between the organic cotton or bamboo sheets. The organic mattress your folks special-ordered for you without flame retardants or other toxins/carcinogens feels divine, and you no longer suffer from headaches and allergies. So far so good. You lean over and crack the window for some cool, fresh air, and shut your eyes and breathe easy—seeing how it's all connected—your good mood, your higher energy, your health, and the health of the world around you. Being green really *can* be a natural part of teenage life—and a defining characteristic of the latest, greatest generation—Generation Green.

Sweet dreams, you green teen!

Tosh has created a fun online test you can take to gauge your level of green, greener, and greenest on a daily or weekly basis. Log on to www.generationgreenthebook.com and click on the Tosh Green Challenge button to see how you're doing.

LINDA'S ACKNOWLEDGMENTS

Can't write a book about saving the planet without thanking *her* . . . our Earth Mama. This is a mere drop in the water barrel, but you know where to find me.

To Tosh—my greatest blessing. Thank you for walking this path with me, and keeping me forever laughing!

My sister, Carol Allen, the rock of my world. Life is so much better with you around! Brother Bill and Mom Dorothy, thank you for loving me and our T-Man so totally.

Mom Etta Sivertsen, Kim, Jose, AJ, and Olivia Vera, and Jerry and Cindy Sivertsen—I love my family and cherish our time together! My ex, Mark Sivertsen, for saying yes to building our green wilderness home. It was a lifetime ago and just yesterday, raising our jungle boy amidst the trees and under the stars. What an amazing adventure!

My best friend, Diane Chandler. Your fierce loyalty and hilarious daily calls fuel me. Hubby Chris—you're the gold standard, baby! Ryann, I'm so proud to be your godmom, and will follow you, Skye, and Brynn anywhere.

Brooke and Kerry McGonigal, our soft place to land. There are no words.

I worship my sistas from another motha: Kelly Van Patter, Rhonda Britten, Val Hoverson, Amelia Kinkade, Andrea Quinn, Lisa Petersen, Nancy Rainford, Nancy Pimental, Susan Andreoni, Arielle Ford, Dina McBride, Gina Turner, Terri Kuykendall, Catherine Oxenberg, Meredith Brooks, Victoria Loveland-Coen, Chellie Campbell, and Linda Northrup—and all my many tennis buds! And Sherry Lansing, Linda Gray,

Barbara George, and Kay Grace, my smokin' hot adoptive mamas. You're all so incredible!

Agent Jenoyne Adams—bringing us this book the day after Tosh shot a green teen video. Crazy cool! Jim Levine, at Levine Greenberg, thank you for wrapping your arms and agency around us!

Sangeeta Mehta, our eagle-eyed editor. You asked all the right questions, girl, and brought the vision. Bless you! To Annette Pollert for so skillfully taking us to the finish line! We adore our Simon Pulse team: Bess Braswell, Bethany Buck, Jennifer Klonsky, Lucille Rettino, Michael del Rosario, Nicole Russo, Carolyn Pohmer, Kelly Stocks, Michael Frost, Jessica Sonkin, Jane Archer, Katherine Devendorf, and Bara MacNeill, among them.

Brilliant magical door opener, Paul Bassis, one of the best! Our *fun,* inspired Live Earth buds: David de Rothschild, Kit Hawkins, and Richard Goldberg.

Leeza Gibbons—for being there and nourishing my green dreams for *forever*! I'm humbled to sit across the microphone from you for our Green Hollywood spots. You're *the* master. Duncan Christy and Katherine Clark, my editors at Delta's *Sky* magazine's Green Scene department. Susie Levan, my longtime editor at *Balance* magazine, bless you for saying yes to covering the green gals.

Lord Robin Russell, it's been over two decades and I still hang on your every-beautiful-brilliant-British-green word. Kreigh Hampbell, my jack-of-all-save-the-world-trades comrade, for your insightful research and enlightened input. You always make me better!

My Wonder Woman assistant, Virginia Arnold. All single

working moms should be so blessed! To Faye Snyder and Stacy Moya for keeping us levelheaded! Judy Sandra, your research skills are spot-on and so incredibly appreciated. Jean-Noel Bassior and Anthony Chiorazzi, in hurricane winds and through late nights you researched and interviewed teens and delivered above and beyond under tight deadlines. I'm so grateful for your sense of fun *and* constant professionalism!

Daryl Hannah; Julia Butterfly Hill; Carol Alt; Ed Begley, Jr. for welcoming us into your trenches. Coldplay, Alicia Keys, John Mayer, and Bruce Springsteen for rockin' the solitary hours no writer can escape. James Arthur Ray for changing absolutely *everything*! I thank God for you!

Ron Maga—LAFD, Angel Craig Wallace for "unconditional," and the cavalry—Burky (Michael Burkhardt), Mike Lee, Brenden Kinkade, Rick Hupp, Michael Higgins, David Kelsey, David Harder, Tim Crescenti, Matt Hanover, Doug and Jeff Rago, Chuck Sailor, Bernard Nussbaumer, Dan Tisch, Bobby Smith, Guru Singh, and Joe Parente for being the best of friends.

My home away from home—the Cypress Inn in Carmel, California. *Gonna extend my stay just one more day.* Ha! To Craig and Charles and Andrew and Carla and Khamis and Denny for your unsurpassed care.

Graydon Carter and Amy Gross for setting the bar!

To my dear Elizabeth Rapoport—bless you, mama lion, for all your invaluable feedback! God willing, may we be old ladies together laughing in your kitchen (with Martha Beck, too!), your orange cat of the day—Bodhi IV?—rubbing up against our ankles!

And to Chris Carter for raising the bar in every way I'd hoped for and never imagined!

TOSH'S ACKNOWLEDGMENTS

Ditto to everyone Mom included—a lot of people supported us this year. I've got to include my environmental EPA group at Valencia High, especially our fearless green leader, Hannah Goldner. To all the cool green teens out there doing the work—especially my friend Sam Weiner (the friggin' genius who gave me hope that a certain muscle car I've been drooling over can run on alternative fuels) and his totally great sister Katie Rose for her smart feedback.

To Boise at www.gliving.tv for helping to kick-start this path for me.

To my buds—especially my two best homies, Mike Orshan and Kurt Hoverson—for being the coolest friends and listening to my green lectures. And to India Oxenberg Van Dien for being my sis for life. Oh, and to my agents at Commercial Talent and AKA, and Jerry Silverhardt—you guys rock and are so patient when I'm slammed!

To my mom, the hardest worker I'll ever know. You're a great mom! Thank you for motivating me to do this timely work and helping me to step more lightly on the earth, following in your footprints.

And last but not least, that little ball of fuzz I call a poodle, who is the shizz!

Peace out. Green out!

There are so many fantastic green resources that it's impossible to list them all here. Below is a small smattering of ones we love, but there are oh so many more. Try giving these a look, and then keep your green contact lenses on and see what else you can find out in the big green world!

Some of our favorite green sites

www.begleysbest.com
(Ed Begley, Jr.)

www.cotam.org

www.earthjustice.org

www.ecomall.com

www.ecorazzi.com

www.enn.com

www.dhlovelife.com
(Daryl Hannah)

www.gaiam.com

www.gliving.tv

www.goodlife.com

www.greenmarket.com

www.greenmaven.com

www.greenopia.com

http://green.yahoo.com

www.grist.org

www.janegoodall.org

www.kellygreendesign.net

www.idealbite.com

www.newleafpaper.com

www.oceana.org

www.realgoods.com

www.rockthevote.org

www.time.com/goinggreen

www.treehugger.com

www.water-ed.org

www.worldwatercouncil.org

www.wylandcleanwaterchallenge.org

A few of the green magazines we love reading

E/The Environmental Magazine

Kiwi

Mother Jones

National Geographic

onearth

Plenty

Sierra

Waterkeeper

Recommended earth-loving green charities, organizations, and resources

Earth Action Network
1536 Crest Drive
Los Angeles, CA 90035
Phone: (310) 203-0162
Fax: (323) 857-1574
E-mail:
earthactionnetwork@earthlink.net
Web: www.earthactionnetwork.org

Earth Island Institute
300 Broadway, Suite 28
San Francisco, CA 94133
Phone: (415) 788-3666
Web: www.earthisland.org

Elephant Family
(saving Asian elephants)
81 Gower Street
London WC1E 6HJ
Phone: (+44) (0)20 7580 3184
Web: www.elephantfamily.org

Environmental Defense
257 Park Avenue South
New York, NY 10010
Phone: (212) 505-2100
Fax: (212) 505-2375
Web: www.edf.org

Environmental Protection Agency
Ariel Rios Building
1200 Pennsylvania Avenue, NW
Washington, DC 20460
Web: www.epa.gov

ForestEthics
One Haight Street, Suite B
San Francisco, CA 94102
Phone: (800) 725-0087
Web: www.forestethics.org

Global Green USA
2218 Main St, 2nd floor
Santa Monica, CA, 90405
Phone: (310) 581-2700
Fax: (310) 581-2702
Web: www.globalgreen.org

Greenpeace
702 H Street, NW
Suite 300
Washington, DC 20001
Phone: (800) 326-0959
Web: www.greenpeace.org/usa

National Climatic Data Center (NCDC)
Federal Building
151 Patton Avenue
Asheville, NC 28801
Phone: (828) 271-4800
Fax: (828) 271-4876
Web: www.ncdc.noaa.gov

Natural Resources Defense Council (NRDC)
40 West 20th Street
New York, NY 10011
Phone: (212) 727-2700
Fax: (212) 727-1773
Web: www.nrdc.org

New York Restoration Project (NYRP)
254 West 31st Street, 10th Floor
New York, NY 10001
Phone: (212) 333-2552
Web: www.nyrp.org

PETA (People for the Ethical Treatment of Animals)
501 Front Street
Norfolk, VA 23510
Phone: (757) 622-PETA
Web: www.peta.org

Rainforest Action Network
221 Pine Street, 5th floor
San Francisco, CA 94104
Phone: (415) 398-4404
Web: www.ran.org

Rainforest Foundation US
32 Broadway, Suite 1614
New York, NY 10004
Phone: (212) 431-9098
Web: www.RainforestFoundation.org

River Keeper
828 South Broadway
Tarrytown, NY 10591
Phone: 800-21-RIVER
Email: info@riverkeeper.org
Web: www.riverkeeper.org

Sierra Club
85 Second Street, 2nd floor
San Francisco, CA 94105
Phone: (415) 977-5500
Fax: (415) 977-5799
Web: www.sierraclub.org

Sierra Student Coalition
600 West 14th St. N.W.,
Suite 750
Washington, DC 20005
Phone: (888) JOIN-SCC
Fax: (202) 637-0410
Web: www.ssc.org

TreePeople (to plant trees)
12601 Mulholland Drive
Beverly Hills, CA 90210
Phone: (818) 753-4600
Fax: (818) 753-8733
Web: www.treepeople.org

U.S. Fish and Wildlife Service
1849 C Street, NW
Washington, DC 20240
Web: www.fws.gov

Waterkeeper Alliance
50 S. Buckhout, Suite 302
Irvington, New York 10533
Phone: (914) 674-0622
E-mail: info1@waterkeeper.org
Web: www.waterkeeper.org

World Wildlife Fund
1250 24th Street, NW
P.O. Box 97180
Washington, DC 20090
Phone: (202) 293-4800
Web: www.worldwildlife.org

Some of our favorite green books (for further study)

Alt, Carol. *Eating in the Raw: A Beginner's Guide to Getting Slimmer, Feeling Healthier, and Looking Younger the Raw-Food Way*. New York: Random House, 2004.

Brown, Lester. *Plan B 2.0: Rescuing a Planet Under Stress and a Civilization in Trouble*. New York: W.W. Norton & Company, Inc., 2006.

Carter, Graydon. *What We've Lost.* New York: Farrar, Straus and Giroux, 2004.

Clark, Duncan, and Unterberger, Richie. *The Rough Guide to Shopping with a Conscience.* New York: Penguin, 2007.

Clinton, Bill. *Giving.* New York: Alfred A. Knopf, 2007.

David, Laurie, and Gordon, Cambria. *The Down-to-Earth Guide to Global Warming*. New York: Scholastic. 2007.

de Rothschild, David. *The Live Earth Global Warming Survival Handbook*. New York: Rodale, 2007.

Gore, Al. *Earth in the Balance.* Boston: Houghton Mifflin, 1992 and 2006.

Gore, Al. *An Inconvenient Truth*. Emmaus, Penn.: Rodale Press, 2006.

Hill, Julia Butterfly. *One Makes the Difference*. San Francisco: HarperSanFrancisco, 2002.

Kingsolver, Barbara, with Steven L. Hopp and Camille Kingsolver. *Animal, Vegetable, Miracle: A Year of Food Life.* New York: HarperCollins, 2007.

McDonough, William, and Braungart, Michael. *Cradle to Cradle.* New York: North Point Press, 2002.

Rogers, Elizabeth, and Kostigen, M. Thomas. *The Green Book: The Everyday Guide to Saving the Planet One Simple Step at a Time.* New York: Three Rivers Press, 2007.

Trask, Crissy. *It's Easy Being Green.* Salt Lake City, Utah: Gibbs Smith, 2006.

Want to DO More?

Join the nation's largest network of young people
committed to solving our environmental crises.

Link up with thousands of students and learn how to
create real change in your life — and in the world.

The Sierra Student Coalition is a
youth-run organization, and
we believe the power to create
change is right in your hands.

You can start making a
difference right now —
Visit www.ssc.org today!

Nonboring, Nonpreachy:
Nonfiction

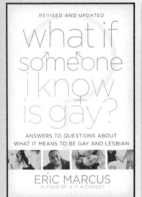

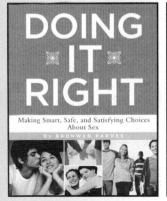

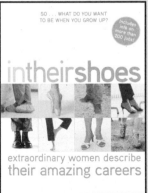

From Simon Pulse | Published by Simon & Schuster